NOBUO SUZUKI

Foreword By Héctor García

Maneki Neko

The Japanese Secret
to Good Luck and Happiness

TRANSLATED FROM SPANISH BY
RUSSELL ANDREW CALVERT

TUTTLE Publishing

Tokyo | Rutland, Vermont | Singapore

CONTENTS

THE THREE CIRCLES OF GOOD LUCK

The most popular Japanese good luck symbol is the *Maneki Neko* (招き猫), the figure of the cat with a raised paw, nowadays found all over the world. There are different legends about where it came from, but it is believed that the raised left paw brings prosperity and good luck. In its right paw, it holds a *koban* (小判), an ancient Japanese coin, and it usually wears a bell around its neck to ward off evil spirits.

Another much loved object that summons good fortune is the *Daruma* (達磨), the figure depicting a monk with neither arms nor legs; people paint an eye on it to make a wish, and then wait for it to come true before painting the second eye.

These are but two of the many symbols and rituals that Japanese culture has for attracting good luck and warding off disasters, such as the traditional aversion for the number four. Associated as it is with death, the Japanese go to such lengths to avoid it that many hotels and hospitals have neither a fourth floor nor a room number four.

Shintoism, Japan's ancestral religion, also has numerous rites for attracting money, love or good fortune, and Buddhism and the animistic religions of territories like Okinawa and Hokkaidō have their own rituals.

How do each of these work and what story or deep meaning is behind each belief? How can we summon up good luck through our daily habits?

This book explores all the tools — some of them magical, others more practical —, mainly from Japanese culture, for attracting good fortune and making our wishes come true. As well as learning the different rituals in an easy and motivating way, we shall explore the essence of good luck and how to incorporate it into our lives with the appropriate habits and attitudes.

I hope to help you bring the Maneki Neko philosophy into your life!

"The day you make your mind up to do it is your lucky day."

JAPANESE PROVERB

FOREWORD

It's been said that Japan is a land of contradictions, and this is true, especially at first sight. I believe this apparent contradictory nature is what makes the Japanese culture so interesting. It can surprise us time and again with discoveries that might seem to make little or no sense. Curious minds experiencing this will want to dig deeper.

When we observe a culture — any culture — as an outsider, we naturally tend to view it through our own preconceptions and biases. If we can't see something clearly through our own lenses, it's easy for us to label it as a cultural quirk. But if we look further, most of the time, we will find wisdom underlying the surface.

When I first came to Japan, I found myself constantly saying things like "Oh wow, that's incredible!" "How is it that this culture is so modern in some ways and so traditional in others?" "Why do people act so rational about some things and so irrational about others?" "Why wouldn't she open my gift in front of me?" And the big one: "I don't understand this approach. Will you explain it to me?"

Asking questions and collecting answers teaches you a lot, and eventually I started writing books about Japanese culture. But after almost twenty years of living here, I have to say that I still know almost nothing. There are many subjects and subtleties about which I am still a beginner. No matter how much I learn, there's always much more to know.

Reading also teaches you a lot, and I am very pleased to introduce you to this new book by Nobuo Suzuki, whose *Wabi Sabi: the Wisdom in Imperfection* remains my favorite book on Japanese aesthetics. In that book Suzuki articulates how a fundamental belief in the necessity of impermanence and imperfection has shaped so much of Japan's art and daily life, So many layers and nuances to explore. And with this new book, Suzuki, has done it again.

Another nuanced and layered subject — one that has remained a mystery to me in many ways — is the role that superstition and luck — or more to the point, the *belief* in luck — plays in this culture. In *Maneki Neko* Suzuki shows how rituals and charms that are meant to attract or preserve luck, or ward off misfortune, are manifestations of something deeper, and how participation in these things contributes to a kind of collective energy.

I always wondered why lucky charms, protection amulets and so on are so popular at the entrance of Shinto shrines and Buddhist temples. *Maneko Neko* explains the purpose these bits of wood, paper or fabric truly serve. Will they ensure the desired outcome, or guarantee that we won't encounter disaster? No. But buying one is an act of optimism, or a statement of commitment to an effort, that does have a very positive effect on us regardless of how things turn out.

By nature, I'm skeptical of anything that smacks of superstition, but when you make your home in a culture so different from your own, you have to keep an open mind and hopefully, the things you participate in out of respect will become things you understand on a deeper level, and you discover that we have more in common with other cultures than we may think. Symbols and tokens of luck and blessing may differ from culture to culture, but their long existence is something most cultures have in common. Rituals and festivals, too, may differ, but the fact that we rely on them as a source of support and celebration is universal.

A while back I had the honor of participating in a Shinto ritual known as *jichinsai*. This is a groundbreaking celebration performed before a house or a building is constructed. During the ceremony, my task was to hit a mound of sand using a big wooden hammer. The *jichinsai* has many purposes: to ask for permission from the *kami* (gods) to construct, to purify the land where the building will stand, to pray for the safety of the workers who will build it, to make sure that it will be completed on time and, finally to ask for a good future in which the people or the businesses that will occupy the new building will prosper.

The *jichinsai* is performed to bless the construction of small houses and skyscrapers alike. Of course, not everything is left to luck; the *kami* are not going to build anything or ensure that the job will be done correctly, but the ceremony helps kickstart a project in which many people will participate in creating something new. It fosters a sense of community, goodwill, cooperation and, again, optimism.

My views on traditions and my definition of superstition have changed over time. I have a more pragmatic understanding these days. I can see the usefulness of our behaviors at different levels. If a belief or tradition helps whoever practices it without hurting anyone else, it's a net gain for all of us. Sometimes it's not even about a practice being useful; it's about the beauty of what makes us human.

Maneki Neko will help you celebrate this beauty. It will enhance your understanding of Japanese culture and entice you to keep digging deeper. It's also the most sensible and uplifting book on luck I've ever read. Every culture has its beliefs about luck, and all of them contribute to our understanding of what we have in common. This book brings Japan's contribution into perfect clarity.

How can we deal with fortune when it shakes our lives either in good or bad directions? Can you create good luck? Can you bring good luck to yourself and your loved ones? How do we deal with bad fortune, which is also inevitable? And what, ultimately, is luck, anyway? These are some of the many questions reflected upon in this book.

I think that believing we'll have good fortune, that all will be well, is a healing outlook in a chaotic world, and that traditions help us to feel more grounded and human. I also think that traditions and beliefs outside of our own have much to share with us, and we have much to gain by digging past their surfaces and getting to know them. This book invites you to do just that.

Dear reader, enjoy reading the words of wisdom in this book. And above all, I wish you good luck! And remember, believing in good luck can increase our chances of having it.

Héctor García
Tokyo 2023

LUCK IS NOT A QUESTION OF CHANCE

I have always been fascinated by the concept of good and bad luck. Ever since I was little, I would ask myself: Why are there some people for whom nothing ever goes right, while others always achieve their objectives? Are there gods out there rewarding some while forgetting about or punishing others? Or is it a simple matter of chance? Either way, it seemed really unfair.

As I grew up, however, I realized there were important differences between the people who chalked all their shortfalls up to bad luck and those who fostered their own good fortune.

The former leave their fate in the hands of outside forces. They hope that good fortune will smile on them, because they do not believe they have the power to influence it. They have a passive attitude and can use up an entire lifetime waiting for the winds to blow favorably.

The latter are those who make every effort to achieve excellent results. They may not always reach their goals, but they try over and again, creating the right circumstances and being alert to opportunities, while fostering mutually beneficial relationships.

We could say that such people apply *ganbatte* to their lives. This Japanese expression translates as "Do your best" and is used to encourage someone who is carrying out a complicated task, or to raise the spirits of someone who is going through a tough time. It is an exhortation to keep on making an effort instead of trusting everything to chance. Far from leaving the result in the hands of fate, as other languages do when wishing "Good luck!" this expression is an invitation to put our all into what we're doing so it turns out as well as possible.

Unsurprisingly, *Ganbatte!* is one of the most loved and frequently used expressions among the Japanese since it encourages us not to give in however great the obstacles may seem.

This perseverance is very much to the fore in the Japanese people's spirit and is behind what is known as "the economic miracle" — the rapid postwar recovery — and their ability to pick themselves up again after each and every natural disaster.

However, the culture of hard work alone is not enough to sketch out the life you have dreamed of. You also need the magic of believing that you can achieve it.

And this is where *Maneki Neko* comes in; the cat raising its paw to attract good fortune — maybe believing, in the way that cats tend to do, that whatever it needs truly is at its beck and call. The rituals and beliefs that mentally predispose us toward favorable scenarios are of great assistance when it comes to shaping our destiny.

For that reason, in this book you will find the most popular beliefs for attracting good luck, along with rites, good luck charms, legendary practices and stories, rounded off with the point of view of leading experts in order to understand how fortune, success and prosperity work.

In these pages, we'll constantly meet a concept of luck that is not a question of chance, but is gently simmered with three ingredients that are essential to Japanese culture:

1. **EFFORT**. Coming back to *ganbatte*, there is no greater fortune than that which we forge ourselves through continuous effort — the famous Japanese *kaizen* —, the basic ingredient for progressing and achieving good results.

2. **WISDOM**. Knowing the keys to success — what makes money flow and what makes you lose it — is the second keystone to good luck. To help you with that, I have included a list of authors and books that have a clear take on this matter.

3. **CONFIDENCE**. If you believe it, you create it, as a popular saying goes. The third ingredient of fortune is having the conviction that what we aspire to is feasible and that we are going to achieve it. There is nothing that we achieve in this world that we haven't first visualized mentally as a real possibility.

With these three ingredients, we are all set to influence our luck and to shape the life we want.

If you read this book carefully and apply just a small part of its rituals, advice and techniques to your life, change will not be long in coming.

Welcome to the Maneki Neko universe!

NOBUO SUZUKI

Throughout this book, we shall take a closer look at many of the following symbols and superstitions:

Japanese good luck symbols and superstitions

Maneki Neko	Cat figures with a raised paw.
Daruma	Figures representing Bodhidharma. You have to paint one of the eyes while setting a goal — the other eye is only filled in when your goal has been achieved.
Omikuji	This is a kind of horoscope written on a slip of paper which shows how lucky you are (*unlucky, par for the course, lucky or very lucky*) and has a few phrases indicating what awaits you.
Ema	Wooden plaques on which you can inscribe your wishes.
Ehomaki	*Sushi maki* which is traditionally to be eaten on *Setsubun* while facing in a particular direction; this direction changes every year.
Koinobori	Carp-shaped streamers that are flown on Children's Day on river banks and in parks. They are a symbol of health and achievement for children. According to legend, a carp that swims upstream can become a dragon.

Omamori	Good luck charms for protection. They are sold in shrines and temples. They tend to specialize in certain kinds of protection, for example, for avoiding problems with your marriage, car accidents, etc.
Hina Matsuri dolls	Dolls that are given out during the *Hina Matsuri* (Girls' Day) celebration. According to mythology, illnesses and bad luck can be transferred from children to the dolls.
Senzaburu	It literally means "A thousand paper cranes." They are decorations that string together a thousand cranes that are folded following the origami tradition. Legend has it that if you fold a thousand origami cranes you may ask the gods to grant any wish and it will come true.
Seeing a spider in the morning	Seeing a spider first thing in the morning is thought to be a good omen.
Big earlobes	The seven gods of fortune have big ears, especially Daikokuten. So it is believed that having big ears brings good luck.

Japanese superstitions associated with bad luck.

The numbers 4 and 9	One of the pronunciations of the number four in Japanese is "shi," which is exactly the same as the word for death. In the case of the number nine, one of the pronunciations is "ku," which is exactly the same as the word for "to suffer."
Whistling at night	Superstition says that if you whistle at night, you will attract snakes. Maybe this is why it is said that in the past thieves and bandits communicated amongst themselves through whistles.
Lying down after eating	"If you lie down to rest after eating, you will turn into a cow," as a popular Japanese saying goes.
Cutting your nails at night	*Yotsume* 夜爪 (cutting your nails at night) is pronounced the same as *yotsume* 世詰め (your death approaches).

THE ETYMOLOGY OF FORTUNE

The Japanese language is rich in words referring to luck and fortune. Throughout these pages, we shall examine the meaning of these words in some depth and look at how they relate to the different traditions that reflect the Japanese people's way of thinking.

For now, a brief introduction to *un* and *fuku*.

運
Un — luck or destiny

The character *un* (運) means luck or destiny. There are many words that use this character to refer to different degrees of luck.

- *Kouun* (幸運): good luck.
- *Kyōun* (強運): very good luck.
- *Fuun* (不運): bad luck.

There is a saying containing the character *un* that the Japanese study at school: *un mo jitsuryoku no uchi* 運も実力のうち. It translates as "Luck is also one of our skills."

福
Fuku — fortune

Fuku (福) is another character that could be translated as "fortune." One of the first words a student of Japanese learns is: *koufuku* (幸福): happiness. It is curious that the word happiness in Japanese contains the character for "fortune."

The expression *fuku wo yobu* (福を呼ぶ) literally means "to find luck." This Japanese expression suggests to us that we can take the initiative and seek out luck rather than just wait for it to come to us.

The new generations of Japanese also use words that have been imported from English:

- *Rakku* ラック is a Japanese adaptation of "luck."
- *Rakki* ラッキー is a Japanese adaptation of "lucky."

THE FOUR TYPES OF GOOD LUCK

*"I notice the harder I work,
the luckier I get."*

CHARLES FRANKLIN KETTERING

The concept of luck has been surrounded by mystery and myth since the dawn of time. But for now, let us go back to the question: Why do some people appear to have more luck than others?

One of the big problems with the word "luck" is that what it refers to may differ from one culture, situation or context to another.

To attract good luck, it is important to understand the difference between various categories and focus our energy on those kinds of luck that we can have an influence on, accepting the rest as circumstances outside our control.

James H. Austin defined four kinds of luck in his book *Chase, Chance, and Creativity: The Lucky Art of Novelty*:

1. **Blind** luck	2. Luck through **perseverance** and **action**
(Outside of our control)	(Partly under our control)

3. Luck through **opportunity hunting**	4. Luck through **invitation**
(Partly under our control)	(Partly under our control)

People with bad fortune tend to obsess over blind luck, which is totally outside our control. On the other hand, the "lucky ones" tend to be experts at attracting luck through perseverance and movement, opportunity hunting and invitation.

Let's delve into the details of these four kinds of luck:

1. Blind luck

This is the kind of luck that happens one hundred percent accidentally. It requires no effort on our part.

Examples of blind luck would be: being born into a wealthy family or not, suffering or not suffering from certain types of illnesses, winning the lottery, having good or bad weather on a trip, etc.

The best strategy, both when blind luck works in our favor and when it works against us, is to accept it when it comes our way.

This is the only kind of luck that is outside of our control.

2. Luck through perseverance and movement

This is the kind of luck that favors us when we learn and work tirelessly, especially when we are always active.

That means you not only have to work within your area of specialty, but also you have to move around to seek out opportunities, learning from those people who are more experienced than you, you have to know much more than your competitors,and get together with those who have other specialties, etc.

The objective of this kind of luck is to create "felicitous accidents" that benefit us, and to achieve it the important thing is not to stand still.

For example, if an artist is always shut up at home, composing and playing music, and never shows anything to the world, never plays in public, nor knows anyone in the industry, that artist is highly unlikely to become well-known.

On the other hand, if a musician, as well as devoting time to composition and practice at home, also starts to perform in public — even if only in small venues —, starts a band where each person specializes in one instrument, goes to other musicians' and artists' concerts and events in their city… Well, very soon "felicitous accidents" will start to occur. Some agent or other might offer to release their music, or someone will invite them to perform in more important concert venues. And what if someone uploads a video of one of their concerts and it goes viral on the Internet?

This type of luck is to a degree under our control. The more we work, not only in the strict sense of the word work, but in the wider sense of making an effort every day to do everything possible to make our dreams come true, the greater the chances are that this luck will favor us.

3. Luck through opportunity hunting

If we are good at detecting opportunities, we will enjoy more success than if we let them go by without even noticing them.

It sounds easy and obvious, but it takes experience and patience.

What is the difference between a good investor and a mediocre one? A good one knows how to differentiate better whether or not it is worth investing in something, but is also good at noticing when to get out of a situation if it ceases to be favorable.

On the other hand, a mediocre one invests in businesses that are destined for failure, and is incapable of detecting the existence of good opportunities. Just as with the mediocre investor, sometimes bad luck comes to us when we get involved in something that isn't right for us.

Training our ability to sniff out good opportunities and ignore the bad ones will increase the chances of our benefiting from this kind of luck. For that, it is important to be competent and to know more than others in our field or passion.

4. Luck through invitation

This is the luck that comes to us when we are invited to be part of unique opportunities that are not offered to others. It is the most difficult kind of luck to attract because it requires a lot of time engaged in networking as well as working on our personality to be special and different from others.

It is a kind of luck that when seen from afar may appear tinged with envy. We may even see it as unfair.

How lucky they are! They always get the best opportunities! Why has he been invited to that private concert and not me? Why have they been hired for that project and not me? That person is famous for being famous, but they don't deserve any credit for it!

Nevertheless, when we get up close to someone who seems to always be connected to this kind of luck, we understand it is not something that happens suddenly, but that this person has worked at it for years and even decades to become a unique person who is a magnet for good opportunities.

Whenever you notice this type of envy-induced questions

bubbling up inside you, turn your feelings around and transform them into curiosity. What has he or she done to get that opportunity that hasn't fallen to me? What could I do to stand out from the crowd and manage to be invited to opportunities that not even he or she would get offered?

Imagine a photographer who specializes in weddings. In their hometown, there are dozens of photographers doing the same job. If they are good, they will be able to make a living at their profession, which is perfectly respectable and honorable. But, if they want to stand out from the others and grow, they will have to behave differently and venture along paths that differentiate them from the rest.

For example, if they learn to speak in public about the art of photography, they will probably start receiving invitations to give lectures on the subject. Another way of standing out would be if, as well as doing wedding portraits, they started to publish nature photos on the Internet. Magazines specializing in that topic would probably start to contact them. And what if they specialize in portraits set in nature?

Perhaps this combination of specialties would be enough to get them a reputation as the number one photographer in their town and to start to get calls from famous people requesting private sessions. This, in turn, will get them new opportunities, which will only come to them and not to other wedding photographers.

Add something special — a secret ingredient — to whatever it is you do. Show off something that no one else has. Thanks to this ingredient, you will end up creating a specialty in which you will be the number one expert in the world.

Once you have achieved this, luck through invitation will be something that will come to you on a virtually daily basis.

What can make you unique so you will be included in opportunities that are not offered to others? What unconventional path could you take so you can start to be incomparable?

As an anonymous saying goes,

> *"Luck is not the criteria of success, but a result of a certain lifestyle."*

GOOD OR BAD LUCK IS NOT DECISIVE

"Things of varying magnitude happen by chance, and little bits of luck, good or bad, are clearly not the decisive things in life. However, when a multitude of great chance events are favorable, life is more blessed, for by their very nature, such events lend it beauty and they are put to noble and good use. Conversely, some chance events crimp and spoil our bliss, for they bring pain and interfere with many things we do. But all the same, even in these instances, nobility shines through whenever someone good-naturedly bears a multitude of great misfortunes, and does so not because he's numb to pain, but because he's noble and great-souled."

Aristotle: Nicomachean Ethics, l.1100b.22-b.32

THE CAT INVITING PEOPLE TO COME IN

This is the literal meaning of Maneki Neko, since Neko is "cat" in Japanese and the verb *maneku* means "to invite in."

It is a talismanic animal that attracts different things depending on which paw it is moving. If it has its left paw raised, it is inviting clients into a business. If the right one is raised, it attracts money.

The bell around its neck helps it to ward off evil spirits.

Maneki Neko is a dynamic representation of the law of attraction, which can be summed up in four steps:

1. **Find out what you want and ask the Universe for it.**
2. **Focus your thoughts on that which you desire through feelings of enthusiasm and gratitude.**
3. **Behave as though what you desire had already been achieved.**
4. **Be open to receiving it.**

I must emphasize that this fourth step is the trickiest because a lot of people know how to give but are not open to receiving. Whether it be because they believe they don't deserve it — perhaps they suffer from imposter syndrome — or because they have poverty neurosis, they remain in need.

On the subject of poverty neurosis, the economist Cristina Benito defines it like this in her book *Money Mindfulness*:

"There are people who deprive themselves of prosperity by not letting money flow toward them (…) Although they could earn money through their talent, they prefer to remain poor and pure, rather than be "sellouts."

These people reject any means that might improve their standard of living, because that would imply betraying themselves. However, poverty neurosis is not the preserve of the anti-establishment crowd, nor of marginalized artists. We also find it in a more veiled way on a daily basis, like with professionals who could get a salary rise or pay rate hike because they have made themselves irreplaceable in their place of work, but don't know how to do it and prefer to keep quiet and wait for those holding the purse strings to take the initiative — something that will never happen. Is it fear of rejection, of failure, or a lack of self-esteem?

In the most extreme cases, what sometimes appears to be a facade of modesty or indifference is in reality hiding a negative message that the poverty neurotic tells themselves unconsciously: I don't deserve any more than I have."

The Cat Inviting People In fights poverty neurosis by reminding us we are deserving of whatever we manage to attract. It is just a matter of asking for it and embracing what life may bring us.

The following two Maneki Neko stories will help us to program ourselves in that direction.

READING THE SIGNS

According to tradition, the origin of the Maneki Neko goes back to some point in the Edo Period (1603-1868). There was a cat called Tama that was usually to be found on the porch of a temple situated to the west of Tokyo. Facing the holy building was an enormous tree.

The tale goes that one stormy day a traveler took refuge under the tree. When Tama saw him, she began to raise her paw over and again to warn him. Surprised by the cat's repeated gesture, the traveler came out from under the tree to approach the cat and see what was going on.

Just then, a great lightning bolt struck the tree and burned it to a crisp.

When he realized the cat had saved his life, the traveler decided to become a patron of the temple for the rest of his life.

This is the most popular story told about the lucky cat, and we shall see a very different version in the next chapter. However, what lesson can we take from this for day-to-day life?

Tama the cat (my cat has the same name) gives the traveler a warning so that he may act quickly and get away from where he is. Thanks to the fact he notices this, the traveler manages to escape from the destructive lightning bolt. It is, therefore, a providential warning.

However, how many times does the universe send us signals that we don't notice?

Whether it be from a cat, a coincidence or any other detail that grabs our attention, we receive extraordinarily valuable signals every day. Observant people, who are alert to life's nuances, grasp these subtle messages that contain great gifts.

This is the reason why there are people who see what no one else sees, and that makes the difference between some lives and others.

If the story of the cat inviting people to come in had happened nowadays, the traveler might well have been playing around with his cell phone under the tree, and wouldn't have noticed Tama's signals. And as a result, he would have been struck down by the lightning bolt.

The Maneki Neko's first message, then, is that **we have to be alert**. Sensing the signals around you allows you to escape danger and capture opportunities.

THE DREAM AND THE FIGURES

"There is luck in what is left over."
JAPANESE PROVERB

There is an alternative story about the origin of the *Maneki Neko* that, strangely, bears no relation the previous one.

It stars Imada, a woman who was so poor she was forced to abandon her cat because she couldn't afford to feed it. Far from feeling resentful toward her, the cat appeared to her in a dream one night and made a peculiar suggestion: that she should make a clay figure of it.

"This will give you the good luck you have not had before now," the cat said to her, and took its leave, raising its paw.

After waking up from this strange dream, Imada got hold of a little clay and strove to carry out what her four-legged friend had told her to do. With her own hands she sculpted the cat just as she had seen it before it faded away — with its paw raised.

Once finished, she placed the figure outside her door so that the sun would dry it out. When the Maneki Neko was ready, the woman was about to take it inside when a passerby took an interest in it and paid her a nice price for it.

This convinced Imada that her cat's promise was true.

With those initial funds, she bought more clay and prepared a dozen or so figures of the cat with a raised paw. While they were still drying out in the sunshine, half of them were reserved by passersby and before long she had sold the other half too.

Imada knew from that day on that she would never go hungry again.

This second story of the origin of the Maneki Neko contains two main messages:

1. **We have to be alert to dreams and other signs that the Universe sends our way because the key to our fortune might be among them.**
2. **It is not enough to get the message; we have to roll up our sleeves in order to make our luck change, as Imada did in the story we have just seen.**

Regarding this last point, **the law of attraction only works if it goes hand in hand with the law of action**. However good an idea may be, in the absence of decisive and constant effort our fortune will remain the same.

BELIEVING IN GOOD LUCK HELPS YOU TO HAVE GOOD LUCK

"I can accept failure,
everyone fails at something.
But I can't accept
not trying."
—MICHAEL JORDAN

Michael Jordan, regarded by many people to be the greatest basketball player of all time, had a lucky pair of shorts. Throughout his career playing for the Chicago Bulls, he kept on wearing this garment from his college days at the University of North Carolina underneath his team's official red stripe.

Another of his famous superstitions was the number twenty-three, which he always wore on his team shirt.

Of course, wearing two pairs of shorts or the number twenty-three on your shirt is not the secret to becoming a legendary player, but maybe believing that it would help him to be lucky gave his confidence a fill-up at key moments.

These days, superstitions are considered to be irrational — simple beliefs based on ignorance that are of no use for anything. But since the dawn of time, we humans have been superstitious. Why? Perhaps because **harboring certain irrational beliefs is useful**.

Even those people who consider themselves highly rational will admit to having beliefs when put to the test. An example is Richard Dawkins, famous for writing books about atheism and rationality, who admitted that although he doesn't believe in ghosts, he would be scared if he slept in a haunted house.

Although rationally we don't believe that haunted houses are full of spirits walking around at night, there is something in our human nature that will make us feel scared. Perhaps it is an evolutionary mechanism to protect us from possible dangers. While there may be no ghosts, sleeping in an unknown place is generally a little riskier than sleeping in one's own home.

Although they are irrational, in some cases and situations, superstitions may help us to behave in a way that is of benefit to us. If it is a superstition associated with something negative, it will dissuade us when it comes to taking unnecessary risks. Whereas, if it is a superstition associated with something positive, maybe it will give us a self-confidence boost that will help us to act in a way that is of benefit to us.

For example, if we have a lucky charm in our desk that we believe helps us when it comes to studying for an exam. Each day, when we see the charm, it will help to remind us that we have to sit down to study. The chances of us actually getting down to it are greater.

According to research by the University of Cologne[1], activating positive thoughts, that is, **believing we are going to be lucky at something, will make us feel more capable**. This will make us act accordingly and we will make more effort to

1. Study by the University of Cologne: http://www.amh.uni-koeln.de/data/dppsenglich/File/PDFSStudien/PsychS21_7.pdf

achieve the desired result. So, the chances of being successful in our endeavor will be higher.

> ### GOLDEN POOP
>
> The golden poop (金のうんこ: Kin no unko) is a symbol of good luck in Japan. The golden poop figures used as lucky charms, some of them with smiling faces, are very popular. The characteristic triangular shape of the golden poop is so likable that in 2014 it was added as an official emoji to the world standard 💩.

In one of the experiments carried out by the University of Cologne, they split the students into two groups. The first group was allowed to have a lucky charm, some object that held sentimental value for them or their favorite cuddly toy, while the other group was not allowed to have anything.

Next, all the participants had to complete a series of exams (mental tests) as well as physical activities in which dexterity was more important than strength.

The students in the first group, the ones who had lucky charms with them during the tests, achieved better results than the ones in the second group!

The conclusion of the research at the University of Cologne is not that, magically, the presence of a lucky charm might solve everything. It is the belief that it is going to help us that affords us greater self-confidence, and gives us an extra boost that offers us an advantage.

Just wearing a pair of blue shorts underneath your other shorts, as Michael Jordan did, will not make you into a great basketball player, but it will inspire you to train more than the rest and will encourage you in a game's key moments.

SUPERSTITION

↓

GOOD LUCK CHARM OR RITUAL WE BELIEVE IN

↓

WE FEEL MORE CAPABLE

↓

GREATER CHANCE OF SUCCESS

TAKARABUNE: THE TREASURE SHIP

According to Japanese folklore, the *Takarabune* (宝船、宝: treasure, 船: ship) is a ship in which the Seven Gods of Fortune journey during the three first days of the year. In the New Year celebrations, it is typical to see paintings, posters, calendars and models depicting the Takarabune.

The legend goes that the Seven Gods of Fortune transport treasure in the ship, which among other things includes: an

The treasure ship with the Seven Gods of Fortune aboard, as imagined by the artist Hiroshige in the nineteenth century. The crane in the sky represents longevity and the turtle in the sea, happiness.

invisibility hat, a purse with an infinite number of coins, rolls of handcrafted brocade fabric, the secret keys for opening the gods' treasure and parchments with texts about how to live wisely.

Japanese engravings (*Ukiyo-e*) of the Takarabune often adorn houses, temples and shrines during New Year celebrations. According to superstition, sleeping with an engraving of the ship of the Seven Gods of Fortune under your pillow helps to get a good first night's sleep of the year.

HATSUYUME AND OSECHI COOKING

Hatsuyume (初夢, 初: first, 夢: dream) is the first dream we have when a new year begins. For the Japanese, it is important to remember it because it is believed to presage the luck you are going to have throughout the year. According to this belief, dreaming about Mount Fuji, hawks or eggplants is a good omen.

Legend has it that these elements bring good luck because Mount Fuji is the highest mountain in Japan, the hawk is a strong, bold bird, and the pronunciation of the word eggplant, "nasu" in Japanese, is a homophone of "nasu" (achieving something).

Along with the first dream, the food we serve to begin the year is greatly symbolic. These first feasts are known as *osechi* cooking and are prepared at the end of the previous year, since it is thought to be an ill omen to cook during the first three days unless it is to make *ozōni*, a soup with *mochi* and stock that is also typical of this festivity.

Osechi cooking is varied and consists of several dishes served in *jūbako* boxes, which are divided into compartments and are reminiscent of *bentō* boxes. Several tiers are put together to create a stacked *jūbako*, which is ideal for taking to relatives' homes and enjoying good omens together.

The *osechi* cooking tradition arose in the Heian Period (794-1185), when dishes started to be prepared with more soy sauce and sugar than was customary so that they would be well preserved for those first three days of the year.

The symbolism associated with the good fortune of the ingredients mainly comes from their pronunciation, as they sound like good wishes in Japanese.

So, *kombu* seaweed always forms a part of the repertoire since it is phonetically very similar to *yorokobu* — being happy. *Kuromame* — black beans — are always included too since *mame* means good health. *Kazunoko* — herring eggs — are eaten so that the new year will bring the family children since *kazu* means number and *ko* is child.

Apart from phonetics, the shape of the food also has favorable connotations for the Japanese; this is why *osechi* also includes, for example, marinated crayfish kebabs in order to "*be able to work a whole lifetime until your back bends like a lobster's.*" Lotus root, a tuber full of holes that is very popular in Japan, is also eaten in the hope of becoming a visionary thanks to those holes you can see through.

Although in the past, each household cooked its own osechi, these days, due to the time needed to prepare it, many families opt to buy it at specialty stores or at the supermarket. While it is a tradition for the shops to be closed for the first three days of the year to allow families to devote themselves to the celebrations, the stores that prepare *osechi* are always bustling.

Everyone wants to be sure of having a prosperous new year thanks to *osechi* food!

THE GOD OF POVERTY AND
THE GOD OF GOOD FORTUNE

Many centuries ago, in a small village in Japan, there lived a very poor man. However hard he strove, he was unable to bring prosperity to his home. His wife would get up at the first ray of sunlight and go to bed at nightfall, working ceaselessly so that they both might prosper.

The trouble was they were unaware of the fact that the God of Poverty lived in their attic, and their efforts were never rewarded with wealth.

Encouraged by his wife's unstoppable spirit, the man worked more hours than ever before. The God of Poverty began to feel uncomfortable in that house.

"What a hardworking couple!" the tenant said to himself, sobbing. "If they carry on like this, I'll have to leave soon."

Such were the couple's efforts that for New Year they were able to muster one or two delicacies to celebrate the important date. Seeing this, the god was in no doubt — it was time for him to leave.

While the couple was eating their modest feast, they started to hear some sobbing noises. Frightened, husband and wife went up to the attic, where the crying was coming from, and found a crestfallen, fragile old man who wouldn't stop crying.

"Who are you and what are you doing in our house?" asked the man, bewildered.

"I am the God of Poverty and I have been living here for years," the distraught god managed to babble, "but you two have been so hard-working on your path that today I will have to go somewhere else. The trouble is no one loves me and I'm not welcome anywhere."

The couple couldn't believe what they were seeing and hearing..

"Don't worry about me — the reward for your efforts is about to arrive," he went on. "Tonight, the God of Fortune will pay you a visit. And then I'll have to leave."

His tears wouldn't stop falling.

The couple looked at one another, realizing that he was the god that had been protecting their house all this time, and that at the end of the day he was a god — what he was the god of didn't matter.

After talking it over with his wife, the man said to the god:

"Since you've been living here such a long time, we'd like you to stay."

"What?!" the god exclaimed incredulously. "But no one loves me!"

"We think it's all right if you live here," the woman confirmed.

The God of Poverty's cry of joy could be heard along the whole street. At that point the New Year chimes began to ring, the moment in Japan when the gods change places. Just then someone knocked at the door.

"Who can that be at this time of night?"

They opened the door cautiously and found themselves face to face with a gleaming, chubby golden god; evidently a bountiful god.

"At last I am here," exclaimed the new god. "I have journeyed from far off lands to bring good fortune to this house as a reward for your hard work."

"It's the God of Good Fortune!" exclaimed the God of Poverty.

"But what is this dirty creature still doing here?" the outraged God of Fortune said when he saw him. "Go away right now if you don't want me to throw you out!"

The burly new arrival made ready to get rid of the fragile body that was "defiling" the house, but was taken completely by surprise by the owners' reaction.

"God of Poverty, *ganbatte*! Don't lose heart!" they said to him.

"But what nonsense is this, you fools?" The God of Fortune couldn't believe his ears. "No one wants this creature in their house — they are all waiting for me!"

Shaking his head in disbelief, Fortune walked away from the house, giving it up as a lost cause.

"We did it!" the couple and the God of Poverty exclaimed as one.

From that day on, the three of them always celebrated New Year together modestly. The household never became materially rich, but was always full of love, happiness and health.

THE SEVEN GODS OF FORTUNE

Seven is the lucky number in Japan and, according to Japanese mythology, that is how many gods of fortune there are, known as *shichifukujin* (七福神).

The Seven Gods of Fortune are:

EBISU: he is the god of prosperity in business and of abundance in harvests, as well as of food in general. He is also the patron saint of fishermen. In works of art, the figure of Ebisu is a fat smiling man with a fishing rod and a fish on his hook who symbolizes the abundance of food. One of the most popular brands of beer in Japan happens to be *Yebisu* (an alternative pronunciation of Ebisu) and the logo is the graphic depiction of this god.

DAIKOKUTEN: he is the god of commerce and prosperity, the patron saint of cooks and farmers. He is the Japanese version of Mahākāla, the Buddhist deity, which in turn comes from Hinduism's Shiva. The legend has it that Saichō, a Japanese monk, traveled to the Tang dynasty in Imperial China at the beginning of the nineteenth century. There he learned about Buddhism, which at that time was spreading throughout Asia. On his return to Kyoto, he climbed to the summit of Mount Hiei and had a vision in which Mahākāla appeared in front of him. After this apparition, Saichō founded the Enryaku-ji temple in Kyoto, dedicated to Mahākāla, but giving it the Japanese name Daikokuten. The figure of this god of fortune is usually depicted as a smiling man carrying on his shoulder a bag full of valuable objects.

BISHAMONTEN: he is the god of fortune in war and battles. As well as being the patron saint of soldiers, he also represents dignity and authority; he protects those who behave according to the rules of society. He is characterized in statues and paintings as a man dressed in armor and a helmet. He sometimes carries a spear in his hand which, according to popular belief, he uses to fight against evil spirits.

BENZAITEN: she is the only woman among the seven deities of good fortune. The goddess of beauty, of talent in arts and music, she is the patron saint of artists, painters, sculptors, writers, dancers and geishas. She appears in works of art as a beautiful woman holding a traditional lute, the *biwa*. Her image is usually accompanied by white snakes or by dragons. The Shintoist shrine on the island of Enoshima, an hour by train from Tokyo, is dedicated to Benzaiten. It is a beautiful place in which the image and symbology of the goddess fill all the corners of the island

Statue of a dragon in the Enoshima shrine dedicated to the goddess Benzaiten.
© Héctor García

Chōzuya (Place for purifying oneself with water at the entrance to shrines) in
Enoshima, adorned by the head of a dragon. © Héctor García

Jurōjin

He is the god of longevity and it is believed that the mythological version is based on a real person who had a very large,
long head and a beard. Artistic portrayals depict him as a tall
old man carrying a cane. He is sometimes accompanied by a
crane or a musk deer. Another element that tends to appear
in his statues is a parchment on which it is said the longevity
of all living creatures is written.

Hotei

Also known as the Smiling Buddha, he is the god of popularity, happiness and good luck. He is also the guardian of children. He is a fat, bald man who always has a smile on his face. He is so obese that his clothes are too small for him and his paunch sticks out revealing his belly button. He usually carries an enormous bag, which is believed to contain good luck for those who believe in his virtues.

Fukurokuju

He is the god of wisdom, wealth, happiness and longevity too, like Jurōjin. His story goes back to a Chinese tale in which a Taoist hermit was able to carry out miracles because he was an incarnation of a star. His origins are similar to those of his companion Jurōjin and sometimes they are confused for one another because they are both represented as old men with beards accompanied by a crane.

THE LAW OF ATTRACTION

"Think that you are lucky.
If you think like that, bit by bit luck will seek you out."
JAPANESE PROVERB

According to this ancestral principle, which became popular at the start of the twenty-first century, you are constructing your reality every single second, even if you are unaware of it. You attract what you are all the time. That is the basis of the Law of Attraction.

The precursor to the idea was the mysterious wise man Hermes Trismegistus who, more than two millennia ago, asserted that *"as within so without."* We attract to our life what we have inside us, just as though we were magnetic.

So, a negative, victim's attitude, which views the world as a place full of danger, condemns us to carry on experiencing just that until there is an internal change toward optimism and empowerment.

As Gandhi said: *"Be the change you wish to see in the world."* Everything begins with you.

The Law of Attraction aspires to change those constricting, internal beliefs for convictions based on abundance. It holds that when you trust in yourself and in the world, fortune comes much more easily. This internal change toward a more optimistic outlook on what surrounds us and on our own possibilities is what indirectly leads to us creating opportunities for ourselves.

Thus, someone who believes themselves to be prepared for a job has a much greater chance of getting the position than someone who, having the same training, feels they don't deserve it.

The Law of Attraction was made popular some years ago by Rhonda Byrne in her book, and later documentary, *The Secret*. However, as pointed out by her numerous critics, Rhonda Byrne merely did an introduction to the workings of the Law of Attraction. She placed a great deal of emphasis on the need to change one's own mentality, without clarifying that it is not just an exercise in faith, but that following this internal change you must start to play your part with concrete actions.

That is, however much you believe you will be able to do something, if you don't work with *kaizen* mentality — the philosophy of continuous progress — nothing will change.

A classic demonstration exercise in the Law of Attraction is the so-called vision panel.

On a piece of cardboard that you may later hang on the wall, you should express all your wishes. You can do it with photos, phrases, drawings, collages, etc. — It's up to you. Expressing your aspirations, whether they be material ones or not, should give your more clarity regarding the course you have fixed for your life. In addition, by seeing it on a daily basis, we will feel the motivation to keep on working for it.

Experts recommend looking at your vision panel every day, feeling the happiness and joy that would come from having already achieved those objectives. That is to say, the Law of Attraction is based on altering your emotional state to shake you out of the deprivation of the *I want to but can't*, and take you to the fulfillment of *I already have everything I want*.

From that point on, your responsibility is to persevere at what you want to achieve while acting convinced that it will happen. The Universe will take care of the rest.

HAPPY-GO-LUCKY

"Luck comes to the doors that laugh."
JAPANESE PROVERB

This adjective defines a happy person who always thinks they are going to be lucky. We often have the idea we must control all aspects of our life, whereas someone who is *Happy-Go-Lucky* acts in a completely opposite way. Rather than trying to control life, these people flow freely with it, accepting whatever comes along, not with resignation but with the certainty that **there is a (good) reason for everything**.

The author and coach Xenia Vives deals with this topic in his book *Tener Suerte en la Vida Depende de Ti* (being lucky in life depends on you). The main message is that **things go better for happy people than for the rest**.

Far from waiting for the outside world to bring them reasons for happiness, a person who has this attitude makes the conscious decision to live happily, irrespective of the external circumstances. This internal happiness is precisely what leads to them receiving good news from the outside.

There is a Japanese saying that goes: *"Where there's a smile, luck arrives."* This could well be the motto of Happy-Go-Lucky people, convinced that a cheerful, friendly attitude will always bring them good news.

One of the foundations of this outlook on life is to renounce complaining, which is a victim's attitude that disempowers us, and to focus our energy on everything that is wrong. As Mother Theresa of Calcutta said, *"Don't call me to go to an anti-war demonstration, call me to go to a peace demonstration."*

In NLP (neuro-linguistic programming) it is said that the mind doesn't understand negative messages, so if we put our energy into something we don't want, in reality, we are empowering and energizing that very thing. On the contrary, focusing on what we desire in a positive way helps us to get it. So, what we are encouraged to do is to have an appreciative outlook on life and to always try to see the best in each situation and person.

Our expectations and prejudices also have an influence on others. So, in line with the so-called Pygmalion Effect, we should treat them as though they were the best possible version of themselves and encourage them to keep going.

People with the Happy-Go-Lucky philosophy are full of this vitality that makes others feel good. They give off positivity and empower others with their confidence in the future.

A simple exercise for beginning to practice this attitude consists of leaving home with the autopilot switched off. Do your route to work as though it was the first time you were doing it. Adopt the *shoshin* spirit — the mind of the beginner. Unhurriedly, look up and marvel at the details of the buildings and trees around you. Explore your world from a new approach, by being curious and appreciative. Then, pay attention to the people and send love to each and every one of them. Observe how that makes you feel.

In essence, **a happy attitude brings your life better results**. Happy-Go-Lucky.

ENERGETIC COACHING

"No one has good or bad luck.
There are people who think they have good luck
and people who think they have bad luck."
—JAPANESE PROVERB

According to the experts in this field, luck and energetic vibration go hand in hand for one simple reason: **we attract what we are**. The whole universe is energy, therefore, the events we may experience will depend on the quality of our energy.

The Japanese author Masaru Emoto demonstrated the effect of personal energy on water in a controversial experiment that he later published in his book *The Hidden Messages in Water*. Emoto divided a few water droplets into two groups. He voiced all kinds of reproaches, insults and hate-filled words over one of the groups. To the other, he devoted words full of love, from a state of deep admiration and compassion. As soon as the water droplets crystallized, the ones in the second group formed beautiful designs worthy of a work of art. However, when he observed the ones in the first group through a microscope, they revealed asymmetric shapes with neither harmony nor beauty.

He concluded that if the energy projected over a few simple water droplets created such a disparity between them, you can just imagine the effect that what we say to one another and the energy we project has on us. At the end of the day, we are sixty percent water.

From this point of view, love, joy, gratitude and Buddhist compassion (wishing the best for everyone) are expressions of high-energy vibration. On the contrary, resentment, rage, selfishness, fear and sadness are low-vibration energies.

The goal of energetic coaching is to climb the ladder from fear to unconditional love, since our vibratory frequency comes from the feelings we harbor inside.

Increasing our energetic vibration can be a lifetime's work, but according to the experts, there are two express routes that can help us to progress at top speed.

1. *Gratitude:* Being grateful for what you have is the first step to escaping from the need that fear generates and, therefore, from low vibration. A good habit for this, each day before you go to bed, is to write down three things you feel grateful for that day. In this way, your brain will get used to looking for things to be grateful for throughout the day.
2. *Wishing everyone well:* There is enough to go around for everyone. We should not fall into the trap of feeling envy or wanting things to go wrong for someone. What we wish others is what we are wishing for ourselves. As one of the Universe's mottoes goes: you get what you give.

THE HONG KONG DRAGON

At the end of the nineteenth century, Tai Hang, today just another neighborhood of the Hong Kong metropolis, was a little fishing village that appeared to be cursed. There were typhoons, plagues, and even an elusive python that finished off a good deal of the area's cattle.

Desperate to find a solution, the inhabitants asked a local fortune-teller for help; he told them the bad luck would go if they celebrated a three-day fire dance.

Prepared to try anything, they found a way to build a straw dragon, which they fitted with 72,000 incense sticks. For three days, the dragon danced through the village, with the help of three hundred people carrying its sixty-seven-meter span.

We shall never know if the fortune-teller hit on the solution, but the fact is the misfortunes stopped. Since then, to be on the safe side, the incense dragon dance is practiced religiously every year.

Some people believe that what was behind the good luck was the amount of incense that was burned. In Buddhist temples throughout Asia it is common to see believers congregated around a metal cauldron, where sticks are burned to attract fortune — the more the better. They are so convinced that this smoke gives off good properties that it is common to see them gesticulating around the cauldron in an attempt to draw all the smoke toward them, as though they could cover themselves with good luck.

Incense has always been attributed the ability to eliminate negative energies and to scare away evil spirits. If we go to a yoga or meditation class it is common to find an incense stick lit, inviting us to leave the heavy burdens of daily life outside and lose ourselves in the state of relaxation and well-being that the burning stick provides.

Given that fire is the element responsible for transfiguring negative energy, burning incense at home is an optimal way to maintain good *feng shui* there. According to experts, rosemary incense is especially recommended for eliminating bad vibrations, as is rosewood and white sage.

In line with the ancestral Chinese tradition, **a lot of energy becomes blocked in room corners**, where two walls meet, so don't forget to thoroughly fumigate there as well. Be sure to **ventilate all your rooms well afterward**, in order to definitively free yourself of everything that should leave.

ZHAOCAI MAO: THE CHINESE GOOD LUCK CAT

*"If you make no mistakes in life,
your life will be a failure."*

—JAPANESE PROVERB

Although each culture likes to think the cat belongs to them, there appears to be a reasonable consensus that the origin of the lucky cat is to be found in Japan.

Even so, the Chinese have their own name for it: Zhaocai (fortunate) Mao (cat).

One of the best-known legends in China about Zhaocai Mao is that of the young Echigoya and his cat Tama, a name that appeared in our first story about the Maneki Neko.

There was a prosperous family business devoted to dyeing fabrics, which was handed down from generation to generation. The business came into the hands of the young Echigoya, who was known for his twin passions: betting shops and his cat Tama.

The young master's servants saw how the family business was going to ruin because of his lack of effort and excessive spending, but he believed it was impossible to lose all of his money since he had so much of it.

Those who saw how Echigoya squandered his fortune day after day were proved right; creditors eventually came to take away all his belongings.

Desperate, Echigoya hugged his cat Tama and asked it to obtain just one gold coin for him as a way of paying him back for all the love he had bestowed on it. After meowing a couple of times on his lap, the cat leaped away and stealthily left the house.

The next morning, it appeared with a gold coin in its mouth. Echigoya was beside himself with joy and ran to the casino to recover his fortune.

At twilight, he returned home having lost everything. Once again, he implored his cat to bring him a coin, promising that this time he would look after it and make good use of it. Tama meowed twice before stealthily leaving the house. And once again, the cat arrived the following morning with another coin in its mouth. Echigoya ran off to the casino, only to return once more with nothing.

"Master, don't you think Tama looks unwell?" the seneschal then asked Echigoya. "He's thinner than usual, and he appears to have no strength."

Indeed, the cat was to be found resting in a corner, clearly weakened. Echigoya hugged him tight and begged him to get better and to go for another gold coin.

"I will use it well this time," the young man promised.

The cat leaped away, this time without meowing, and silently disappeared from the house. Suddenly, Echigoya wondered where his cat was getting the gold coins, so he decided to follow him. He walked stealthily behind Tama as far as the temple and saw how the cat began to pray, in front of the altar, while clapping its paws together and singing:

"Take hands, take feet, give me gold coins! Take belly, take fur, give me gold coins!"

Echigoya couldn't believe his eyes. His cat was literally giving its all to get coins for him. Horrified, he shouted:

"That's enough, Tama, don't do it!"

But the cat, after looking into his eyes for a brief moment, continued with its praying. Little by little, Tama began to disappear, until three gold coins appeared in his place.

It is said that from that day on Echigoya became a new man. He was never seen again in the casino, and worked so hard that with the passing of the years he managed to get his fortune back. In memory of his beloved cat Tama, he had a sculpture made of a cat holding a gold coin at the entrance to his house.

The neighbors began to think that the curious statue was responsible for Echigoya's economic recovery, and they asked for it to also be placed in their houses to attract good fortune, not knowing that the good fortune was the product of a change in the man's heart and of a great effort.

One of the messages of this story is that **our luck will only change when we change our habits, which means, above all, getting rid of our negative ones.**

In China, every little detail of the Zhaocai Mao is important, and the paw the cat raises to wave and welcome people tells us what its function is. If it raises its left paw, it will serve to attract good guests. If it raises its right paw, it will serve to attract money. There is also a small percentage of lucky cats that have both paws raised. In this case, they protect the place where they are located.

FUNERALS FOR THE LIVING

Why wait for reincarnation to start afresh when in Thailand it is possible to experience your own funeral while you are still alive?

This Buddhist practice, which may be carried out in some Thai temples, consists of getting into a white coffin to eliminate negative karma and to get rid of bad luck.

The practitioner lies down in the white coffin, which is the color of death in most Asian countries, and this is covered with a sheet of the same color. Their hands, mimicking the arrangement for the deceased, are placed together on their chest holding a bouquet auspicious herbs or flowers such as orchids.

This practice is considered a kind of rebirth in life through which you may cleanse yourself of all of the negative energy that experiences have built up in you. So, the majority of people who take part in this cult tend to have had bad experiences recently, as though someone had cast the evil eye on them.

Many of them are nervous when they arrive, so the monk's first task is to calm them down and tell them they should focus on the present moment, and try to feel the energetic change that is about to take place. When the ritual is over, the monk blesses them with perfumed holy water.

After this symbolic death, the participants claim to feel their energy has been completely renewed, as though they had been reborn and were starting from scratch from the state of purity we come into the world with. Grateful for this second opportunity, they can begin a new life with far less baggage.

This type of ritual started around 2004 and has become a real phenomenon. While ninety percent of Thais are Buddhist, they don't all take kindly to this new practice. However, those who have experienced it say the effects are automatic, and it can even make a business prosper or help someone to overcome an addiction.

Whether or not bad luck can be repelled with a funeral in life, what is certain is that it reminds us that **death is the only thing we are all heading for, so we should be careful how we live our life.**

INDIAN GOOD LUCK RITUALS

The Japanese are not the only fanatics of lucky charms and superstitions. These beliefs also abound in India, and it is common to see totems and good-luck charms in the most unexpected places.

If you ever have the chance to travel to the subcontinent, it won't take you long to notice that some cars are dragging a couple of old slippers behind them. Far from being an oversight, this is to repel the evil eye.

It all began when cars first appeared, and the evil looks of envy directed at those who could afford to have one created an energy that was too dense for the drivers to handle. Since then, it has been common practice to hang slippers from cars so that their ugliness may repel the evil eye. These days, many truck and taxi drivers opt for simply drawing the outline of a slipper on the back of their vehicle, so as not to drag slippers behind them for thousands of miles.

As in most superstitious cultures, **money also has its own rules: a rounded amount should never be handed over**. For a monetary gift to be auspicious, it should have an extra rupee: for example, 10,001 rupees.

For that reason, many of the money-filled envelopes given as wedding gifts include an extra rupee.

For Indians, it is fundamental to protect the home with favorable gods. No home is without its representation of Ganesha. However, if the home is being renovated, then the goddess you need is Kali, the female energy of the great god Shiva.

In addition, during the Diwali festival, everyone decorates their house with hundreds of lights, waiting for the goddess Lakshmi, who governs wealth and prosperity, to come and stay there.

Other than Hindu rituals, Indians have many superstitions that are common to other cultures, like it being bad luck to see a black cat, to walk under a ladder, to sweep at night or to break a mirror. In these cases, bad luck sticks to the person who has the belief in question.

We are what we do. But we are also what we believe.

EMA

Legend has it that the *kami* — Japanese deities — travel on horseback. In ancient times, wealthy people would donate horses to shrines in the hope that would bring their families good fortune.

People who couldn't afford this gift began to donate horse-shaped wooden plaques. Over time, the custom of writing wishes on these plaques spread and, instead of having a horse shape, they started to imitate the silhouette of a stable with a triangular roof.

These origins explain the name of these plaques, which are called *ema* (絵: drawing, 馬: horse).

These days, depending on the shrine and the year, the plaques not only have drawings of horses, but also of mythological creatures. Custom dictates that you have to write your wish on an *ema* and hang it up at the shrine. After some time, all the plaques are burned, liberating the spirit which is believed to live in each of the wishes.

If you travel to Japan, you can write your wishes on an *ema* when you visit a Shintoist shrine. If not, you can also write down your wishes or goals in your favorite notebook or on a post-it or something similar and stick it to your fridge.

According Dr. Gail Matthews (Dominican University of California) in her study "The Impact of Commitment, Accountability, and Written Goals on Goal Achievement," **writing down our goals increases our chances of achieving them by roughly forty-two percent**.

While writing down our goals in not guarantee of success, it has been proved that this practice is of great help for different reasons:

- The act of writing helps us to clarify what is dancing around inside our mind.
- It serves as a reminder to us each day to focus our energy on what is truly important to us.
- Psychologically, when we write down our goals, it is as though we were signing a contract with ourselves. It helps us to be more committed when it comes to taking the initiative to carry them out.

Practical exercise. Our personal *ema*

First step:
Choose an area of your life in which you currently feel an emptiness or need to take the initiative to correct something:

1) Love and relations
2) Money, finance
3) Goal and/or work
4) Health
5) Learning and personal growth

Second step:
In reference to the topic chosen in the first step, write down several phrases with the first thing that comes into your head,

regardless of the order. They may contain feelings of frustration about the area of your life you want to correct.

Third step:
Change what you have written in the second step into at most three specific goals or actions. They must be positive and proactive. Write them down on a sheet of paper you can hang on your wall next to your desk or on the fridge — somewhere you can see it every day.

Practical example:
Step 1) We choose the topic **Health**.

Step 2) We write down the first thing that comes into our mind: over the last few years I've been letting myself go and I've put on weight. Each time I resolve to control my dietary habits, I fail miserably. I can't remember the last time I took any exercise. I should start to activate myself and take more care with my diet.

Step 3) We write **three goals** down neatly on a sheet of paper:

- Exercise at least twice a week, starting with yoga sessions.
- Give up candy and desserts.
- The goal and ultimate wish is to lose ten pounds in the next six months.

Woman reading ema plaques at a shrine in Tokyo. © Hector Garcia

Ema plaques in Hakone, adorned with dragons, a mythological creature that often features in local legends. © Hector Garcia

ONE HUNDRED PERCENT RESPONSIBILITY

Continuing our exploration of good fortune, we will leave Japan behind and set sail for some islands that are halfway between Asia and America, although geographically speaking they are located in Oceania.

Present-day Hawaiian culture has a lot of very different influences, including Japan. In fact, one of its most famous contemporary authors (who we will meet in later, dedicated chapter) is Robert Toru Kiyosaki, the conference speaker and businessman of Japanese descent who wrote *Rich Dad Poor Dad*.

In this chapter, though, we shall talk about the ancient Hawaiian wisdom, known to many people as Hoʻoponopono, one of the foundations of which is **the principle of 100% responsibility**.

This culture's *Kahunas* — which may be translated as masters or priests— state that **each human being is one hundred percent responsible for their own reality**. Therefore, it is useless to blame other people, the world's ills or any other external situation for the position we are in.

Each person creates their own reality. Therefore, if you don't like yours, **you are one hundred percent responsible for creating one that makes you happy and fulfilled**.

Ho'oponopono means **"to correct an error,"** which makes a lot of sense, given that if we accept that we have the power to create our own reality — even if until now we have acted unconsciously — we also have the power to change it.

The moment someone accepts that, deep down, everything depends on oneself, they stop blaming circumstances and others and set to working at their life. From that point on, being lucky or unlucky is a personal choice.

Let's look at a couple of examples of what changes when we assume one hundred percent responsibility.

- If you have been "unlucky" in love up until now, ask yourself who it was that picked your partners, most likely incurring in the same mistakes over and again. Who does changing that come down to?
- If things have not gone well for you financially until now, but they have for other people you know, ask yourself what they do that you don't. Once again, who does change depend on?

You can apply the principle of one hundred percent responsibility to all aspects of your life, starting from the premise that **everything is created in your mind before it becomes a reality**. So, by changing the way you think and act, you totally change your fate.

On a more spiritual level, Ho'oponopono holds that painful, negative memories are stored in the subconscious and produce illness and pain. Until we "clean" them, we will continue to repeat the same painful episodes and circumstances, because we are attracting them from our subconscious.

For this cleaning, the Hawaiians use a string of four expressions: **Forgive me, I'm sorry, I love you, Thank you.**

Forgive me initiates liberation — it yanks out the anchor of guilt.

I'm sorry offers our acceptance of responsibility for what has happened.

I love you opens the doors of the heart, expressing the connection between oneself, others and the universe.

Thank you switches on the energy of abundance, by recognizing everything we already have.

When faced with any conflict or pain that is causing us suffering, Ho'oponopono recommends several repetitions of **Forgive me, I'm sorry, I love you, Thank you** to wipe our mental field clean of negative remains and to create the life we want from a position of one hundred percent responsibility.

DOES LUCK EXIST?

Nassim Nicolas Taleb wrote *Fooled by Randomness: The Hidden Role of Chance in Life and in the Markets* in 2001, six years before the publication of his very famous and widely-translated *The Black Swan*.

In this second book, the essayist and former broker expounded on those highly improbable events — black swans — that radically alter their surroundings when they occur. For Taleb, 9/11 or the success of Google and YouTube are examples of black swans, and he argued that these disruptive events will be ever more common. Undoubtedly, Coronavirus and the rise of TikTok are proof of that.

In the book that concerns us, focused specifically on the topic of luck, Taleb invites us to realize that **the world is governed by chaos, randomness and non-causality**. Therefore, when we describe an investor as a visionary, we are forgetting about the part that chance has to play in the result.

Due to retrospective bias and, especially, survival bias, we tend to forget about the many who fail, and to remember the few who succeed and then to create reasons and patterns to explain their success, without admitting it was in large part fortuitous. Not everything is as logical and predictable as we would like to see it *a posteriori*, when we try to establish causes that are often impossible to prove.

According to Taleb, **commonplace success may be put down to effort and perseverance, but a large scale success tends to have a lot to do with variation and luck**.

In Taleb's opinion, the very randomness that the book title refers to — and not logic — governs the nature of many everyday happenings or events in the business world.

So, *Fooled by Randomness* narrates in essay form how fortune, uncertainty, probability, human error, risk and decision-making work hand in hand to influence our actions, the business context, and more specifically, investments, and reveals how the role of chance in our lives is much more important than we would like to admit.

If you realize you are doing something extraordinarily well in a random situation, keep on doing what works for you, but restrict your possible losses. There is nothing wrong with taking advantage of randomness, as long as you protect yourself from negative random events. Many people did very well out of selling masks during the first year of the pandemic. The problem came when demand fell and they didn't find a substitute product to maintain their turnover.

Randomness means there are some strategies that work well for any given cycle, but these cycles tend to be short or medium-term successes, and might not be the best in the long term. They are suboptimal strategies, which gain a randomly beneficial short-term cycle. Suboptimal strategies and characteristics may appear to be desirable in the short term, although in the long term they will be unsustainable.

In any case, the key to knowing whether it is an ability of yours or just randomness is repeatability. **If you cannot repeat it, then it is just chance, so there is no ability involved.**

Taleb claims we make decisions based on our bias, which is emotional. Neither the detection of risks nor the avoidance of them are processed by the rational part of the brain, rather they largely stem from the emotional part. The consequences are enormous: it means that **rational thought has very little to do with risk avoidance**. Oftentimes, the only thing we do is try to rationalize decisions we have made at an emotional level with some kind of logic.

The crux of this book could well be the idea that the only aspect of your life that fortune doesn't wield control over is your behavior (which is more emotional than you thought it was). Everything else has an element of chance.

Even so, Taleb states:

"Those who were unlucky in life in spite of their skills would eventually rise. The lucky fool might have benefited from some luck in life; over the longer run he would slowly converge to the state of a less-lucky idiot…"

—NASSIM NICHOLAS TALEB, FOOLED BY RANDOMNESS: THE HIDDEN ROLE OF CHANCE IN LIFE AND IN THE MARKETS

"All of life bewilders.
Nothing in it secure,
And chance takes it off course.
Hope cheers the heart,
But exactly what's to come,
And which way one's carried,
No mortal knows.
A god guides all… and yet,
Often, some terrible breeze,
Blows against good luck."
HERMOLOCHUS: FR. 846 (PMG)

RISK AND WHAT WE CAN CONTROL

According to Stoicism, **worrying about things outside of our control is the source of unhappiness**. Seneca, one of the most important Roman Stoic philosophers, said:

"Luck is what happens when preparation comes across an opportunity."

That is, "being ready" is under our control. We can always improve our readiness in order to be prepared whenever an opportunity comes along. According to this viewpoint, we can "create" or "manipulate" part of "general luck," but another aspect of luck (opportunities) is outside of our control.

A useful way to think about luck is to divide it up following this Stoic philosophy depending on the problem we may be facing.

For example, if we are studying for an exam, ninety percent or more of luck is in our hands if we prepare well for it. If we don't study, maybe that drops to fifty percent or less. It is our responsibility to study as well as we can to minimize the percentage we leave to pure chance.

The level of luck we can manipulate in our favor when it comes to finding a partner is less flexible. However friendly we might be, perhaps the other person won't like us, and this is a factor we cannot control.

When it comes to health issues, if we lead a healthy life — eating well and doing exercise — the chances of not falling ill increase, but there is still the possibility of being struck by ill fortune, which is outside of our control. Your responsibility is to focus on what you can control, that is, on maintaining a good lifestyle free from stress.

If we play the lottery, or if we like betting, the only thing we can control is our taking part — the rest is in the hands of fate. 99.9999999% or more is outside of our control.

If you are a pilot or someone working in a high-risk profession, you have to make sure that 99.9999999% is under your control, and leave hardly anything to pure chance.

With these examples, I would like you to reflect on different facets of your life in which you can have a degree of influence on the percentages you can control and those in which you can't.

There is nothing wrong with throwing yourself into situations in which almost everything is in the hands of pure chance, but it is important to analyze and be aware of the situation.

You can choose the risk level suitable for your personality.

"High risk, high reward," as they say to motivate entrepreneurs when they found a startup.

Useful questions for weighing up our entrepreneurial and risk-taking capacities:

- Roughly what percentage of this new life path or challenge is under my control?
- How can I best prepare myself in order to minimize my chances of having bad luck?

- What is the worst thing that can happen if I am struck by bad luck? What is the best thing that can happen if everything goes well?
- Can we try it again even if everything goes wrong? If you invest all your money in a company and it goes bust, you will be ruined, but if you only invest one percent of your money, even if you lose it, you will be able to try again.

CHANCE FAVORS A PREPARED MIND

French microbiologist and chemist Louis Pasteur famously said: *"In the field of observation, chance only favors prepared minds."* This goes hand in hand with what Seneca said about the meeting of preparation and opportunity.

Over time, the often-quoted maxim transcended science and is summarized as:

Chance favors a prepared mind.

Pasteur, one of the most important scientists of all time, wanted to put across the idea that scientific discoveries and advancements only happen if we have the necessary knowledge for them.

With the passing of time, we tend to have a romantic vision of geniuses and imagine them creating new theories purely by chance. Take the example of Isaac Newton who saw the apple fall and suddenly had the eureka moment that led him to develop the law of universal gravitation. To reach the point at which he had the intuition to connect the falling apple to a new law of physics, Newton studied and experimented for over forty years.

Yes, eureka moments, chance and luck exist, but we often forget about all the knowledge and preparation that leads to a magical moment.

There are some kinds of luck that we cannot choose; for example, where we are born, or certain health-related misfortunes, but with many other things in life, we are the ones responsible for taking the necessary steps to prepare ourselves the best we can and, consequently, to make luck start to work in our favor.

"How lucky everyone is except me!" says the lazybones lounging on the sofa watching the news as he sees how someone has successfully sold a company or won an Olympic medal.

In Japanese, we have this maxim:

"Chance does not smile on those who are not prepared."
偶然は準備のできていないものには微笑まない

Yamamoto Tsunemoto, a Buddhist monk who lived in the Edo era, wrote this in the *Hagakure*:

There is disparity in the military tactics and strategy (gungaku) demonstrated by men who are prepared, and those who are not. The prepared warrior is not only able to solve problems in a quick and commendable fashion by virtue of his life experience, but he can react appropriately through his comprehension of measures to meet any scenario. He is always ready. The unprepared warrior lacks foresight, and even if he succeeds in solving a problem, it is merely through good fortune rather than good planning. A warrior who doesn't think things through beforehand will be ill-equipped.

Tsunemoto recognizes that luck may sometimes even help someone who is not duly prepared, but clearly considers that **whoever builds up wisdom and experience has an advantage over the rest.**

GOOD LUCK

A couple of decades ago, two Spanish business consultants, Àlex Rovira and Fernando Trías de Bes, were successful in Japan and in around thirty other countries with their tale *La Buena Suerte ("Good luck")*.

The story begins with two old friends who bump into each other in a park after not having seen one other for a long time. The two men's "luck" could hardly be any more disparate.

The first one had won the lottery and, after leaving the village, things went from bad to worse for him until he ended up ruined.

The second man had very modest beginnings, the complete opposite of his childhood friend's. He started working as a caretaker, but ended up creating an empire. He managed it without any "strokes of luck" or inheritance.

"How did you manage it?" the first man asks him, fascinated.

The other answered that it was thanks to a tale his father passed on to him, which begins like this:

"A long time ago, in a faraway kingdom, there lived a wizard called Merlin who had all the local knights gather in the grounds of the royal castle and said to them:

'For a long time, many of you have been asking me for a challenge. Some have suggested I organize a tournament among all the knights of the realm. Others have asked me to organize a jousting and sword fighting contest. However, I am going to propose a different challenge.'

The expectation among the knights was at fever pitch. Merlin went on:

'I have learned that in our kingdom, seven moon phases from now, the Magic Shamrock will sprout forth.'

This caused a commotion, murmuring and exclamations among those present. Some already knew what he was referring to — others did not. Merlin restored order.

'Quiet down, quiet down! Let me explain to you what the Magic Shamrock is: it is a unique four-leaf clover that gives he who possesses it a unique power too — unlimited luck. It will last forever and may be used in any sphere of life. It brings luck in combat, luck in commerce, luck in love, luck in wealth... unlimited luck!'"

The Ten Laws of Good Luck are taken from the tale, and we shall see some of the key points from them here:

- The first is that *"Luck doesn't last long, because it doesn't depend on you. You create Good Luck yourself — this is why it lasts forever."*
- In order to create our own Good Luck, we need to create new circumstances that make it more likely for good things to happen.
- This creation of favorable circumstances depends on preparation. **PREPARATION + OPPORTUNITY = GOOD LUCK.**

- "No one can sell luck," the authors claim. "Good Luck is not for sale. Distrust good luck merchants."
- Opportunities are not a question of luck or chance, as many people erroneously believe. They are always out there. The difference is that some people know how to see them and others don't.

This modern self-help classic also conceals an idea we have seen at various stages in this book. **Successful people are not from another planet — what makes the difference are their habits and attitude.**

So, the key question is: **What do they do that I don't?**

WARASHIBE CHŌJA

Once upon a time, there was a young man called Yosaku, who would go from village to village helping other farmers and living off the food he received in exchange for his work. Since he had no home, he used to sleep in Buddhist temples, where he prayed to Kannon, the Goddess of Mercy.

"Kannon, I work very hard every day. Please, let me sleep here tonight and allow me to find work tomorrow," he would say in his daily prayers.

One night, Kannon, bathed radiantly in golden light, appeared beside Yosaku.

"Wake up," the goddess said to him. "The way you live your life is worthy of my unbridled admiration, Yosaku. You have nothing, but never complain and help others in exchange for nothing more than a few vegetables by way of food. I want to help you build a happy life. Remember this well: the first thing you pick up tomorrow morning will bring you great fortune."

With those words, Kannon disappeared.

The following day, on his way to work, Yosaku tripped over a stone and fell. When he stood up, he saw that a stem of straw had stuck to his hand. "Might this be what Kannon was talking about? How will this bit of straw bring me fortune?" he thought, bewildered.

While he was puzzling over this, a horsefly flew by and began to buzz around his face. Yosaku caught it and tied it to the end of the straw. The insect tried to escape, but the young man held on to the other end of the straw, as a result of which the horsefly made the straw twirl around in circles, like some kind of amusing toy.

A rich child who was passing by saw it and couldn't help himself:

"I want one! I want one!" he said to his guardian.

Yosaku was quite happy to give it to him, and in exchange he was given three oranges.

"Wow, three oranges just for a piece of straw!" he thought contentedly, and once more carried on his way.

Soon afterward, he came across a woman who appeared to be in quite some distress.

"I'm so thirsty I think I'm going to faint! Please, give me a little water," the woman said to him.

"These oranges might help you. Please take them," he said to her, offering her the three pieces of fruit he had just acquired.

The woman ate them and soon felt better.

"You've saved me — I'm very grateful to you. Please, take this as a sign of my gratitude," she said, handing Yosaku a packet of silk fabric.

"This expensive fabric must be Kannon's gift," thought Yosaku, who was starting to believe in the goddess's prophesy.

After walking a few more yards, he came across two samurai who had halted in the middle of the path. Their horse, overcome by heat exhaustion, was lying on the ground, unable to get up.

"What a useless horse!" said one of the samurai, who couldn't get the horse to move.

Yosaku observed the scene for a while, before coming to a decision:

"Honorable samurai, would you like to swap your horse for this woven silk fabric?"

The samurai couldn't believe his luck.

"Wonderful! Today must be our lucky day. Not only can we get rid of this useless horse, but you will also give us a bundle of silk!"

Yosaku turned to the horse and understood that it suffered from the same problem that the woman had experienced earlier. It needed water urgently. Looking around, Yosaku saw a small stream, sufficient to calm the animal's distress.

"Here, drink a little water," he said to it, wetting its muzzle with the water he had carried.

Yosaku had to make a good few trips to the stream, but finally the horse stood up, its distress eased. Yosaku then got on the horse and rode to the outskirts of the next town, where he came across a country house. He noticed that the owners were getting ready to set off on a trip, and were piling a lot of baggage onto a cart, so he thought they might need another horse.

Yosaku went up to the man who seemed to be the owner of the house and, after telling him about his journey, asked him if he would like to buy the horse.

"I'd love to buy it, but I'm going on a trip and I don't have any extra money. But how about you keep part of my paddy field instead? And you can look after the house while I'm away."

Yosaku not only got his own rice paddy, but also a place to live. This inspired him to work harder than ever.

A few months later, the owner returned from his trip. The rice was thriving and the house had been cleaned inside and out, including the facade. It had never before appeared so majestic. The owner was impressed with Yosaku's work.

"You've left me speechless," he told him. "You're a good lad, honest and hardworking. Why don't you marry my daughter and live in this house forever?"

Yosaku couldn't believe his luck. He happily accepted, got married and was blessed with adorable children. He always worked very hard and became very rich. There was always room in his heart for the poor and the needy, who he helped in the hope they might prosper as he had.

Everyone knew his story and they called him *Warashibe Chōja*, literally "the straw stem man."

Bodhidharma, the 5th-6th century CE monk credited with the founding of Zen Buddhism and the transmission of Chen Buddhism to China, is the model for the Daruma doll. Two legends are behind this connection. One is that Bodhidharma sat so long in still meditation that his arms and legs dropped off from lack of use. The other is that, having fallen asleep during meditation, he cut off his eyelids so as to force himself to remain awake. Thus, the Daruma doll is wide-eyed and limbless.

If you strive, something will be achieved—it may not be the goal you had hoped to achieve, but every striving is a journey. Every striving teaches us more about ourselves. Regardless, it's traditional to burn the year's Daruma before obtaining a new one. Here, a crowd watches their dolls burn at the local temple. The journey will resume or start fresh with a new Daruma, a new filled-in eye. So when you fill in the first eye, get ready to move forward with an open mind. At the end of the year, you may find that you achieved something more valuable than the goal you started with. And so it is up to you to fill in the other eye, or not.

Daruma with one eye filled in. The hollow figure is weighted at the bottom, like a tumbler doll. Knock him down and he rises again and again. The dolls are often accompanied by the phrase "Nanakoro-bi ya oki" (七転日 や お き: "Down seven times, up eight.") In this way, Daruma links good fortune to resilience and persistence. Bodhidarma was said to have owned nothing but his red robe, so Daruma most commonly wears red (for overall good luck), but he also comes in other colors representing different types of goals (p.2 bottom): green for health, orange for mental pursuits, white for emotional and spiritual well-being, and so on.

Here we have Maneki Neko, the "beckoning cat" (招き猫) herself. She stands outside of business of all kinds, and can be found inside homes, fashioned into accessories and jewelry, embroidered into clothing, and in so many other iterations. She usually holds the oval-shaped koban coin circulated during the Edo period. The phrase on the coin, "sen man ryou" (千万両), means "10 million gold pieces."

Other versions of Neko may hold a carp (a symbol of abundance), a money pouch, a fan or drum (the latter, especially, symbolizes burgeoning business). A raised right paw brings luck and wealth. A raised left paw invites customers into places of business. Or, she may raise both paws to protect the business or home and those within it. Like Daruma, she comes in different colors—white for optimism and purity, red for happiness in relationships, black for protection from evil, and so on. She rarely goes without a neck ornament of some kind—most frequently, the bell that tells you where she is at all times.

Besides being a symbol of luck, she is a symbol of welcome—of connection—and as a talisman universally loved by her people, she adds to a sense of commonality and community.

The Omikuji (お み く じ) are a sort of lottery ticket and "fortune paper" that you can find at your local Shinto shrine or Buddhist temple. These random fortunes predict your chances of good luck, happy relationships, success, avoidance of disaster and so on. It is customary to affix a bad Omikuji to a wall of wires or a pine tree on the shrine or temple grounds, as a way of leaving the bad fortune behind rather than allowing it to cling to you. If your fortune is a good one, you may want to carry it with you, or you may choose to tie it on the tree or wire to increase its positive effects. The Omikuji is steeped in poetry, as it consists of one hundred short, prophetic quatrains. Its history dates back to the Heian period, and it's enjoyed today as a tradition—another of the threads that bind people together, and connect them to their past.

Another interpretation behind Maneko Neko's beckoning paw derives from an Edo-period story about a feudal lord led to safety from a destructive storm by a cat beckoning with its paw, leading him to Gotokuji Temple (Tokyo). The monk of the temple gave the lord shelter and hospitality and the lord gave the temple land and rice. Thousands of cats can be seen at the temple today, most particularly surrounding a relief carving of Kannon, bodhisattva of compassion. In this legend, luck and prosperity are the result of kindness.

The carp—or koi—is a symbol of prosperity and abundance. Bred now to adorn ponds and garden pools, carp have long served as a food source. They, like daruma, are a symbol of determination and perseverance and the pursuit of a goal. Japan and China share a myth that if a carp swims upstream and jumps the waterfall, it is rewarded for its strenuous efforts by being transformed into a dragon. For this reason, carp streamers are flown on Children's Day (May 5)—to encourage children to keep striving. Once again, good luck is associated with a positive attitude and hard work.

Omamori (お守り) is the term given to various types of amulets often dedicated to specific Shinto kami or Buddhist bodhisattva and are intended to give blessing in a particular situation or endeavor, rather like the medal of a particular patron saint. They most often take the form of a small cloth bag into which the wearer or giver may place a prayer or meaningful object. It becomes a symbol of the wearer's goals or the giver's encouragement. They are generally purchased or given at the start of the new year, and "retired" or returned to the place where they were purchased when their purpose has been fulfilled.

Ema (絵馬) are prayer plaques that are purchased then hung at Shinto shrines and Buddhist temples. Visitors write their prayers and wishes on them, and leave them in the gods' hands by hanging them in a dedicated area of the shrine or temple. Writing on an ema serves as a kind of unburdening and outreach, and reading the ema of another is yet another thread that connects us with understanding and fellow feeling.

Both Eastern and Western cultures love the crane. They represent everything from magic and the elements to purity and immortality. In Japan, they are the "bird of happiness" and symbolize peace, wisdom, longevity and luck. Graceful, majestic, and faithful to their mates and to their home, they are said to live 1000 years. The senbazuru (千羽鶴) associates the crane with patient work, as the senbazuru consists of 1000 folded origami cranes strung together. It is believed that a person who folds 1000 cranes will be granted a wish.

The Shihimai 獅子舞 (Lion Dance) is a fixture at festivals all over Japan. In the Tsukiji district of Tokyo, the Lion Dance has a festival of its own, the Tsukiji Shishi Matsuri, which is held every three years in June. As in other parts of the East, the lion dances to draw good fortune, protect the people against evil, and be a source of energy and exuberance. Festival goers line up to receive a good luck bite on the head.

It's not only the lion who dances during festivals. Group dance is an integral part of matsuri, as these festivals are an act of community, of coming together to celebrate, to ask for good luck and protection, and to give thanks. Coming together in joy, entreaty and gratitude is yet another act that brings out the best in people and fosters a positive atmosphere and attitude—one of the best ways to encourage positive outcomes.

A benign sort of money laundering. The secluded Zeniarai Benten Shrine houses a natural spring. It is believed that money washed in its water will multiply. Founded in 1185, this small shrine in Kamakura, Kanagawa Prefecture is largely Shinto, with a bit of Buddhism mixed in. Like so many other holy places, its story involves a visit by a god in a dream. Ugakufujin, the kami the shrine honors, is a god of the waters, whose identity became merged with that of the Buddhist goddess Benzaiten (also called Sarasvati). Collectively they became associated with a prosperous harvest. The money-washing tradition came a bit later, in 1257, when Kamakura's ruler Hōjō Tokiyori first washed his coins in the spring's waters.

Poop as symbol of luck is based simply on sound. In "kin no unko"—Golden Poo—the "un" sound in "unko" matches the "un" sound in kōun o—the word for "good luck." From this little pun have come pendants, toys, figures, emojis and the icing on cupcakes. The flame sculpture atop the Tokyo's Asahi Beer Hall has been nicknamed "kin no unko," for obvious reasons.

The seven lucky gods (七福神, shichifukujin) have origins in India and China as well as in Japan. They act much like patron saints in Christian faiths—each has a specialty. Often depicted together, it is comforting to think of them as working together for our benefit. The number seven is itself considered lucky in Japan.

Nearly all the lucky gods have their origins in Buddhism or Taoism but Ebisu—god of fishing, agriculture, commerce and honest hard work—is Japanese to the core, and much loved in this archipelago where fish are a major source of nourishment both for people and economy. He is usually depicted with a fishing pole in one hand and a sea bream or carp in the other. Note his large ears and long earlobes, which are said to be a feature of those blessed with a lucky nature.

Benzaiten is both Shinto and Buddhist, with roots in India. She is the goddess of wisdom, good fortune and all that flows—water, knowledge, wealth, human relations, time. As one who spans a number of regions and religions, she can be relied upon for a broad worldview, a deep understanding, and the spread of compassion. Nearly always pictured with her stringed instrument called the *biwa*, she is the muse of musicians.

Fukurokuju, whose origins are in China, represents the Southern Polestar, and as such is a source of guidance. His name (福禄寿) combines happiness (fuku) and wealth (roku) along with longevity (ju), so he can be looked to for these blessings as well. He is sometimes depicted with animals symbolizing longevity, such as a turtle, crane or black deer, or any combination thereof. He is characterized by his long beard, the sign of his old age, and his elongated bald head, in which he stores the wisdom of the ages. This sage carries a staff— perhaps of a wanderer, perhaps of a hermit, perhaps, as befits his years, as a cane to propel him through the daily lives of his adoring disciples. This is yet another example of the association of luck with wisdom—it's hard not to recognize their constant pairing in Japanese culture.

Bishamonten (毘沙門天) (or Bishamon (毘沙門)), who comes originally form India, is the guardian of the gate, the protector of temples, worshipers, and their gifts. In this role, he is prepared for battle. In one hand he carries a spear, in the other the pagoda that is the divine treasure house where he stores divine offerings and from which he bestows them. Therefore, Bishamonten is also a god of good fortune, a giver of blessings. He also goes by the name Tamonten (多聞天), which means "listening to many teachings." Believers of any and all faiths are under his protection.

Jurojin (寿老人), grandson of Furorokuju, shares many of his grandfather's characteristics. He too is a god of longevity, often accompanied by a crane, turtle or black deer. He too carries a staff and he too is a representation of the Southern Polestar. It is even said that grandfather and grandson often occupy the same body. He is said to be based upon a Daoist mystic who was given deity status after his death by being more or less grafted onto Fukurokuju and therefore doesn't have any real following outside of his role and status as one of the seven lucky gods.

Daikokuten (大黒天) is the patron of the risk-takers, the bold carvers of their own fortunes and destinies. He smiles on all who move bravely forward, be they honest people of business or thieves and cheaters. Originally a Hindu war god, he became over time a cheerful deity presiding over Japanese kitchens as the god of the five grains. He has been represented in several forms, including a female form. As god of agriculture—vital to all people and a mainstay of most economies—his blessings are sought by just about everyone. He is generally depicted with a mallet in his hand and a bale of rice beneath his feet. He is sometimes accompanied by a mouse or rat because where there is grain, there are rodents.

Hotei (布袋) has been given many names by many cultures. He is said to be based on a Chinese Buddhist monk named Budai who gave away all he had, keeping only the robe he wore. So complete was his giving, so pure his enlightenment, that he passed through life without harm and without worry. In his perfect simplicity, he received abundance. He is the god of contentment and the guardian of children. Carved figures of Hotei depict him sitting, standing, lying down—however he is positioned, he is always smiling. This "laughing Buddha" is loved in both East and West, and many a Hotei statue's belly has been rubbed as a call for luck or expression of gratitude.

SADAKO AND THE THOUSAND PEACE CRANES

"Carrying on gives you strength."
—JAPANESE PROVERB

As a young girl, Sadako Sasaki was a victim of the atomic bomb that the United States dropped on Hiroshima in 1945. On the day of the tragedy, she was two years old. Her house was less than a mile from the impact zone. At the moment of impact, the blast wave hit her so hard she was knocked flying out of the window. Her mother ran to look for her, supposing she had died, but miraculously she didn't have a scratch on her.

Sadako had as normal a childhood as could be expected and became a member of her school's relay running team. But when she reached the age of twelve, she was diagnosed with leukemia, caused by nuclear radiation, and they told her she had barely months to live.

A friend told her of a legend that said that if you create a thousand origami cranes, any wish will come true. In the hospital room, she began to fold paper to create one crane after another.

As recounted in the book *The Complete Story of Sadako Sasaki* (Tuttle Publishing), co-written by her older brother Masahiro and the artist Sue DiCicco, as the days went by, she lost strength and found it harder and harder to fold new cranes, but she managed to pass the thousand milestone, getting as far as one thousand three hundred origami cranes before the day of her death.

Her wish didn't come true, but it gave her hope in her final days of suffering, and her story became a symbol of peace.

After her death, a statue of Sadako holding a golden crane was erected in the Hiroshima Peace Memorial Park. And not only in Japan — a statue dedicated to her was also built in Seattle's Peace Park.

Each year on August 6th — Peace Day in Japan —children from all over the country fold origami cranes in honor of all the children who have been the victims of war. The schools in Hiroshima take the cranes to the Peace Memorial Park, where thousands of them are hung up near Sadako's statue.

Her story teaches us that, although superstitions and beliefs do not perform miracles, they do have the power to become symbols of hope. Sadako's cranes are a reminder that humanity can create a better future — a world with peace.

Hope is one of the best healing elements for the human heart. As Anne Frank said, *"While there's hope, there's life."*

THE LESSONS OF THE RICH FATHER

"Don't look back, don't look back,
there are no dreams behind you."
—JAPANESE PROVERB

Hawaii is home to the author and consultant of Japanese descent Robert Kiyosaki, who became famous at the end of the twentieth century with his work *Rich Dad Poor Dad*, which begins like this:

"I had two fathers, one rich one poor. One was intelligent and very polite; he had a doctorate (...) The other father never finished high school (…) one of them had financial problems his whole life. The other became one of the richest men in Hawaii."

So as not to create spoilers, I'll leave it to your imagination and judgment to guess which of the two made a fortune, which one became the rich dad. I will focus on how he managed to shape his own good luck.

One of the book's principles is that **selling your time in exchange for money is terrible business**, since, according to Kiyosaki, *"The only difference between a rich person and a poor one is how they use their time."*

Our time is limited, and what we can get in exchange for it is only enough to make ends meet or to continually get into debt.

This is what Kiyosaki refers to as **"the rat race."** That is, people spend the whole month working and rushing around to pay the bills and pay off their loans at the end of the month, after which the wheel starts to turn all over again.

If we are lucky enough to get a promotion or a pay rise, we automatically increase our spending, thus continuing to be in debt, and the rat race carries on endlessly. In Kiyosaki's words:

"An important difference is that the rich buy luxuries last, while the poor and the middle classes tend to buy luxuries first."

How can we leave the rat race and change our luck?

According to Kiyosaki, it's all about getting assets that can work for us. Here are some examples:

- Investing in real estate that generates rent.
- Automating businesses that produce profits without us needing to be present (for example, an online course).
- Having shares that pay dividends each year.
- Earning royalties for jobs we have already done; this is the case of a writer who earns profits each year from their book sales.

In Kiyosaki's opinion, **our wealth is measured in the number of days we can live off our assets**. Following that argument, a professional earning $25,000 a month but whose expenses come to the same is poorer than someone who has current savings of $25,000 and can get by on $2,500 a month.

The former cannot last even one month without working, while the latter can go ten months without earning money and therefore is much richer.

In any case, the philosophy behind having assets not requiring our presence is that they should generate recurring income, over and above the savings we might build up.

For Kiyosaki, "It can't be done" is one of those forbidden phrases and he explains why:

"The phrase 'It can't be done' makes strong people weak, blinds people who can see, makes happy people sad, converts the brave into cowards, deprives a genius of their shrewdness, makes rich people think like paupers, and limits the achievements of the great person residing inside all of us."

What can you do to become a rich dad?

THE THREE CIRCLES OF GOOD LUCK

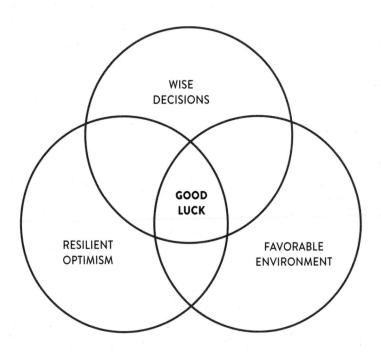

THE FIRST CIRCLE OF GOOD LUCK: WISE DECISIONS

Making good decisions is of vital importance. The repercussions of a bad decision may have consequences for many years. On the other hand, if we choose well, the winds of chance will start to blow in our favor.

For example, choosing a good partner to share our life with is a choice that will make us grow as people. On the other hand, if we get it wrong, a partner who is not compatible with our life plans may pull us under even if they don't mean to.

The big question is: how do we make good decisions? Here are **three keys** that will help you in moments of doubt:

1 – Choose whatever gives us the most optionality

"Optionality" is a term often used in the investment world to refer to investment opportunities where a financial product may be acquired and, in the future, you have the option, but not the obligation, to sell.

Faced with several options, it is always better to choose the one that might open more doors for us in the future and doesn't force us to do anything. For example, if you make the decision to educate yourself and learn something new, you will have more job opportunities, and perhaps you will stop feeling forced to work in something you don't like just to make money.

A good decision has the ability to give you more options in the future; on the other hand, a bad decision closes the doors to you, and, potentially, will make you feel trapped in a lifestyle you don't like.

The key question is: **Does this give me more or less freedom?**

2 – Be flexible like bamboo

We human beings tend to get stressed out when we have to make vital decisions. Something that can help us to take the weight off is to think of solutions that are at the same time flexible and whose course we can correct in the future.

Bamboo is capable of bending in bad weather without breaking. It is flexible and adapts to environmental conditions. You can also be like bamboo, adapting yourself to sea changes.

Do you have a plan B? And a plan C? Is it in your interest to rent or buy a house? If you buy, will you later find it easy to sell?

3 – Strong emotions are your number one enemy

If you make decisions when you are sad, tired, angry, anxious, stressed out or drunk, later on, when you are thinking clearly, you will realize you made a mistake and will regret it.

Strong emotions are the number one enemy when it comes to making decisions. They cloud our ability to see the situation with clarity.

The best leaders tend to be people who know how to separate their emotions from their decision-making.

If it is not a good emotional time for you, don't be in a hurry to make a decision — take your time.

Go on a trip to your favorite place or devote an afternoon to your favorite hobby. Go for a long walk, treat yourself to a dip in the sea, contemplate the dusk... When you are feeling relaxed, think about your dilemma again; now is the time to listen to your intuition and perhaps an alternative solution will emerge as though by magic.

If you still can't manage to disentangle your emotions, explain your situation to friends and relatives so that they can give you their take on it.

In Japan, in the business world, we use what we call the "Ringi System" for making decisions—that is, seeking consensus among many people. **The *ringi* forces everyone to be aware of the change that is going to be carried out and they all have to give their "approval" for it to be carried forward.** It takes time to achieve a consensus through *ringi*, but it helps to avoid any personal bias being introduced.

When it comes to making personal decisions, we don't need to be as extreme as the Japanese *ringi* system. It is always good to talk to other people to find out what they think about our situation — not to allow them to decide for us, but to open our mind to new points of view. We are the ones who will have to be responsible and live with the consequences of our final decision.

Table for helping you to make vital decisions wisely: answer questions 1 to 3 both for Choice A and B.

	Choice A	Choice B
1 – Optionality: will it open doors to me in the future?		
2 – Flexibility: will it allow me to change course in the future?		
3 – Intuition: what does my heart tell me?		

Other questions that can help us when faced with indecision. Write each question on a card or *post-it* and consider them from time to time.

- Which decision increases my chances of luck being on my side and of good things happening to me?
- What is the worst thing that could happen? And the best?
- Consider the completely opposite option. Do you like it? Do you dislike it?
- Do you feel overwhelming excitement?
- Does it align with your life ideals?
- What would the person or people you most admire do in your place?

- Do I only have option A or B? Maybe I could consider an option C.
- What will my life be like a couple of years from now if I follow this path?

THE SECOND CIRCLE OF GOOD LUCK: RESILIENT OPTIMISM

Do optimists have better luck?

No one is immune to bad luck. Bad things will happen in our lives — it is inevitable. But within our control is the way we react to these events. If we react like a pessimist, it will be difficult for us to shake off our bad luck; if, on the other hand, we choose optimism, the chances of everything getting better will be greater.

The next time someone says to you "You're a lucky person," you can answer: "I'm an optimist."

Optimism has been studied, especially concerning illnesses and recovery. The results are clear: **optimists get better much faster and their mortality rate is lower.**

We all know the saying about the glass that is either half full or half empty. But let's take a look at other, more concrete ways of talking about optimism. Let's go a little deeper into ways of defining optimism so we may better know how to identify if we are falling into a pessimist's mentality or not.

In the nineties, Martin Seligman introduced the concept of "**explanatory style.**" According to Seligman, **a person may be an optimist or a pessimist depending on how they explain to themselves the things that happen to them in their life.**

Seligman classified the "explanatory styles" into three dimensions:

1) **Temporal vs Permanent:**
   - Optimists tend to explain negative events in their lives as "temporal."
   - On the other hand, pessimists attribute "permanence" to any bad thing that happens to them.

2) **Specific vs Universal:**
   - Optimists explain the bad things that happen to them as "specific" events that probably won't happen again.
   - While pessimists refer to "universal" explanations for things outside of their control that will happen again precisely because they are "universal."

3) **External vs Internal:**
   - Optimists tend not to blame themselves in excess, that is to say, they explain what has happened as something "external" to them.
   - On the other hand, pessimists blame themselves; their explanations are "internal."

To sum up, the explanatory styles may be:
   - **Optimistic if it is Temporal, Specific and External.**
   - **Pessimistic if it is Permanent, Universal and Internal.**

After having lost their job, the pessimist will say they will never again be able to find something as good (Permanent explanation); they will also speak ill of the work situation in the world generally and say how unfair everything is (Universal explanation); and finally, they will blame themselves for not having the talent for anything (Internal explanation).

Whereas an optimistic person will say they will soon find a new job that is better than the previous one (Temporary explanation), since what has happened is a one-off and probably won't happen to them again (Specific explanation), and it was the company's financial situation that forced them to make redundancies (External explanation).

Why is the explanatory style important?

One of the most effective ways to deal with setbacks or traumatic events in life is to not lose hope and not blame yourself.

Notice that, in the case of the pessimist who has lost hope of finding a job, they expect the future to be worse than the past. Whereas the optimist doesn't lose hope in their future being better.

Has something bad happened to you lately? What is your explanation for this event? Is it a pessimist's explanation (Permanent, universal, internal) or an optimist's (Temporal, specific, external)?

THE THIRD CIRCLE OF GOOD LUCK: A FAVORABLE ENVIRONMENT

One of Jim Rohn's most famous phrases is: **"we are the average of the five people we spend the most time with."** In saying that, he was trying to bring our attention to the importance of having people around us who benefit us. If all our friends and relatives are overweight, it will be really hard for us not to be so. If they are all poor and unemployed, it won't be easy for us to get a job and earn money.

The best strategy is to **surround ourselves with the kind of people who have similar ideals to our own about how to lead a good life**. This will help us have a greater chance of things turning out in line with the future we imagine. Some will say we were lucky, but we will know that one of the most important factors behind our success was that we had good traveling companions at our side, who helped us in both the good times and the bad.

What Jim Rohn said may seem like an exaggeration, but later studies have confirmed the wisdom of his maxim.

According to Nicholas A. Chistakis and James H. Fowler's conclusions in *Connected: The Surprising Power of Our Social Networks and How They Shape Our Lives*, after analyzing data from several studies, the effect goes further, and doesn't only come from the five people closest to us in our day-to-day.

According to their analysis, if a friend of yours is very overweight, you have a forty-five percent higher chance of putting weight on in the following years. What is more, if a friend of a friend is obese, the chances of you putting weight on are twenty percent higher than if your friend's friend didn't exist.

Yes, even if you don't know them personally! The effect also spreads to friends of friends of friends; in this case, the risk of putting weight on is ten percent higher.

That means that not only your friends contribute to you gaining weight, but also their friends and their friends' friends.

The results of the studies are clear, but how is it possible for us to be affected by a person we don't even know? The answer to that question is still being investigated since there are many factors that intervene. But it appears that it has to do with what we perceive as "acceptable" or "unacceptable."

If all the people we live with drink alcohol at all times of the day, we will perceive it as something normal and, therefore, in order to integrate ourselves into the group, we will also submit to peer pressure to follow the same behavior and will end up with an addiction, because it is something "accepted" by everyone we know.

On the other hand, if our social circle has a balanced diet and exercises regularly, if we want to feel like one of the crowd, we will also tend to eat well and exercise.

As well as being aware of the fact our social circle affects our behavior in a positive or negative way, we should also take into account that we too are one of those five people who are important to others. So, we should set an example, raising the average score of those five people as much as we can.

The best way to change other people is by setting an example.

The best leaders are those who lead by example rather than just giving orders.

There are many things in our environment that perhaps we cannot control: the place we are born, our family circumstances, health problems, etc. However, what we can always control is our attitude and how we act, setting an example for the rest.

If you are friendly, your friends will start to be friendlier. And the effect will spread! Bit by bit, we can all create a friendlier world.

How to look after our social environment

It will be very useful to ask yourself these questions and reflect on some of the following ideas:

- Does this person who has invited me to have a coffee boost my energy or drain it?
- When it comes time to say goodbye to someone after we've been on a long journey together or had a coffee, do I wish I could spend more time with them? Do I have the feeling I don't want a meeting to end, or on the contrary, am I wishing for it to end from the moment it starts?
- Am I spending too much time with this person or too little time with someone I should be paying more attention to?
- If I was my friend, how would I like to be treated?
- Rescue your loved ones — don't dump them at the first opportunity; help them to overcome their troubles by setting an example.

- Your true friends, those who really want the best for you, will always tell you the truth, however hard it may be. Accept their constructive *feedback*.
- There will be people who approach you because they want something in exchange. There is nothing intrinsically bad in that, but we must understand that relationships based solely on transactions are not true friendships; they operate without the heart, just like a business. Learn to differentiate between the two types of relationships to avoid upsets.

FORTUNE COOKIES

Almost everyone has held one in their hands at one time or another. After desserts and coffee, the waiter brings a fortune cookie, that little horseshoe-shaped wafer biscuit containing a personal message such as...

Stop procrastinating — start today.

Only you can bring about that change.

Adjust your gaze: you may see things very differently.

Fortune cookies are made with flour, vanilla, sugar and sesame oil. Although many people associate them with Chinese restaurants in the United States, everything points to them having originated in Japan.

They were probably created by Japanese immigrants in California between the late nineteenth and early twentieth centuries.

Their precursor in the nineteenth century may have been a biscuit native to Kyoto that contained an *omikuji*, the strips of paper that predict the future that we mentioned in the table in the book's preface. These biscuits are a little bigger and darker, and are still sold in a few regions of Japan, and in Kyoto's *Fushimi Inari-taisha* temple.

There is a debate about who was the first person to serve the modern fortune cookie. The first to claim this honor was Makoto Hagiwara, the owner of San Francisco's Golden Gate Park Japanese Tea Garden, and the cookies came from the Japanese patisserie Benkyodo. The tradition began at some indeterminate time between 1890 and 1900.

After the Second World War, the fortune cookie industry passed from the Japanese to the Chinese who were settled in the United States, who took advantage of the fact that one hundred thousand Japanese Americans — among them, pastry chefs — were sent to internment camps.

Until the early twentieth century, these cookies were handmade. When Shuck Yee invented the fortune cookie maker in Oakland, it created a great reduction in costs and allowed the cookie to spread to all the Chinese restaurants, and later to Europe.

Nowadays, the biggest manufacturer of these fortune cookies is in Brooklyn; the company is called Wonton Food and produces four and a half million units a day.

For a lunch or dinner with friends, it is a good idea to serve our own fortune cookies after the meal, introducing messages we have written ourselves or taken from our favorite authors. Although it is quite laborious to prepare, there are tutorials on YouTube that are easy for anyone to follow.

Whatever the message may be that you found in a fortune cookie, if it resonates with you and you think it can help you to implement a relevant change, there are several things you can do:

- Keep the slip of paper with the message on in your wallet, so that you "stumble" on it now and again as a reminder.
- Take a photo of the message and put it as your wallpaper on your cellphone or computer, until you feel you have fulfilled what the message asked you to do.
- Write the message on a sheet of paper or in a notebook and each day note down underneath it something you have done to honor the motto, until you feel you have incorporated it into your life.

A written message, like the ones found in a fortune cookie, may be the beginning of an important change in our life, but that change will only take place if we accompany it with concrete actions to influence our fortune.

KIT KAT: THE LUCKY CHOCOLATE BAR

The famous American chocolate bar arrived in Japan in the early seventies and became a hit within the space of a few short months. One of the main reasons was its name, which in Japanese is pronounced *kitto katto*, very similar to the Japanese expression *kitto katsu*, which means "I'm sure we're going to win."

It wasn't long before the Kit Kat became something symbolic to give as a gift to a student before an exam as an auspicious object. It was regarded as some kind of lucky charm for getting through the exam smoothly.

Kit Kat soon exploited the lucky coincidence that its name in Japan was pronounced almost exactly like that victory phrase. The company began to promote the product in adverts as a lucky charm, claiming that one in three students got a Kit Kat before an important exam.

The chocolate bar became so popular that, even today, Japan is the country with the widest variety of Kit Kat flavors in the world. We can find it in matcha tea, strawberry, cheesecake, wheat, cookie, pure cocoa, peach, melon, pistachio, mango, orange, raspberry, banana and caramel, passion fruit, apple, sweet potato and even sparkling wine flavor, to give just a few examples.

The explosion of flavors began in 2004, when the green tea variety was introduced, taking the whole country by storm. Since then, the selection has kept on growing, reaching over three hundred different flavors in less than twenty years, some of which were just limited editions available only for a short time.

In 2014, Kit Kat achieved the impossible: unseating Meiji, the largest confectionery company in Japan, as the number one seller in the whole country.

It is commonplace to find assortment boxes of Kit Kat. They are ideal gifts for someone whose tastes you don't know well, but who you want to wish good luck.

If you travel to Japan, make sure you bring back special flavors of Kit Kat as a gift for friends and family who like candy — you're sure to see a look of surprise on their faces with some of the stranger varieties.

Once more, the main thing is **the ritual that gives us the confidence that we are going to pass the test.**

COLONEL SANDERS' CURSE AND NARRATIVE FALLACIES

In 1985, the Hanshin Tigers, a baseball team from Kansai, came first in the Central League. To celebrate, the fans gathered at the Dotombori Canal and decided that people who looked like one or other of the players should begin jumping into the water.

They found reasonable lookalikes for all the players and began jumping into the canal, but they couldn't find anyone who looked like Randy Bass, the Hanshin Tigers' bearded American batter. Drunk on euphoria, they came to the logical conclusion that a statue of Colonel Sanders, the founder of the KFC restaurant chain, who, like Bass, also had a beard, would be the perfect candidate.

The fans stole the Colonel Sanders statue from a nearby KFC restaurant and threw it in the canal.

Superstition has it that this act of vandalism brought a curse upon the Hanshin Tigers. Over the following years, they always lost the championships and the urban legend began to go around that "until they fished the Colonel Sanders statue out of the bottom of the canal, the Hanshin Tigers would not be able to rise to the championship again."

At the end of the eighties, a group of divers tried unsuccessfully to find it. In the nineties, the baseball team continued to fail to achieve victory.

In 2009, during the construction of a footbridge over the canal, Osaka municipal workers found the remains of the statue by chance.

After twenty-four years sunk at the bottom of the water-way, its color had faded, but even so they cleaned it up and purified it at a Shintoist shrine to eliminate the supposed curse. Then it was put back on display at the entrance to a KFC restaurant near Hanshin Tigers' stadium.

But, over the following years, the baseball team kept on losing. They soon came to the conclusion that, despite being out of the canal, the curse was still active. The directors of the baseball team and of the KFC restaurant chain agreed to take the statue to Tokyo.

They put it inside the KFC offices in the capital, closed to the public, but in a place where the employees of the restaurant chain could see the famous statue and take photos of themselves next to it. Nevertheless, despite it being far from Kansai, the Hanshin Tigers kept on losing.

The KFC executives decided the ultimate solution would be to lock it up in a room so that no one could see it.

In 2014, the Hanshin Tigers started winning again and finished first in the Central League once more.

The Colonel Sanders statue was then released from its confinement and returned to Kansai in 2017. Now, instead of being considered a cursed statue, it is believed to be a good luck talisman.

That is how the Japanese tend to tell the story of the cursed Colonel Sanders, but it is not entirely true. In order to justify the story's rationale, they avoid mentioning the fol-lowing facts:

- They threw the statue in the canal the day they celebrated winning the Central League in 1985, but fifteen days later they won the final of the Japan Series. They won even with the statue lost beneath the water.
- People only began to talk about the curse in 1988, when a television presenter said: "The Hanshin Tigers won't win again until the Colonel Sanders statue is found." Until then, no one seemed to care about the statue.
- The Hanshin Tigers won the Central League in 2005, when it still hadn't been found.
- As of today, the year 2022, the Hanshin Tigers still haven't won the Japan Series. That is to say, despite having freed themselves of the supposed curse, they have only managed to win the Central League, but still haven't won the Series (the most important title in Japan) since their victory in 1985, fifteen days after they threw the statue in the canal.

Seen in the light of this new data, it would seem poor old Colonel Sanders has nothing to do with how well or how badly the Hanshin Tigers play baseball.

Urban legends, popular beliefs and, in general, any story that tries to explain past events tend to fall into the trap of the "**narrative fallacy.**" This is what we call **the human tendency to explain past events as an inevitable sequence of causes and effects, when in most cases what happened was random.**

Telling stories, even if they fall within the category of narrative fallacies, helps human beings to explain their lives and how the world works. Even so, it is important to be aware of the risks, since we have a tendency to only see the facts that fit in with the story we want to tell (no one mentions the victory in the Japan Series when they tell the Colonel Sanders tale) and to manipulate the way we explain the past, seeking logical connections that perhaps do not exist in reality, in order to justify what happened.

Stories that fall into the trap of narrative fallacies may even become dangerous when they are used as a tool to try to manipulate others or as a basis for predicting the future. This is common in modern journalism, especially when giving explanations for economic or financial changes.

On a personal level, used correctly, without falling into negativity or trying to predict the future on the basis of the past, spinning stories to explain things that happen in our lives is a beneficial thing. **Narrative fallacies help us to put certain events in order so as to free ourselves mentally and thereby be in a position to deal with our daily life**.

For example, explanations like these, although maybe not one hundred percent true, will help us psychologically: "I got divorced because *a*, *b* and *c* happened," "I decided to leave my job because of *a*, *b* and *c*," "I've found the perfect person for me because *a*, *b* and *c*."

On the contrary, explanations that try to predict the future on the basis of what happened to us in the past, such as: "I've failed math three times — I'll always be bad at math," "I've split up with my last few partners — I'll never find someone who is right for me," will not help us in the slightest.

Just as the Colonel Sanders statue does not have the power to decide the Hanshin Tigers' fate, **do not allow an explanation of certain events from your past to become a belief that limits your future possibilities**.

THE PORTUGUESE COACH'S CURSE AND THE SELF-FULFILLING PROPHESIES

Many sporting curses and superstitions may fall into the category of self-fulfilling prophecies. When, after being sacked, the coach Bela Guttman said: "Without me, Benfica will never win another European Cup" he had the power to make both Benfica players and fans "believe" it. More than half a century later, they still haven't won a European Cup. Maybe they need someone to tell them the curse has been lifted?

TETRAPHOBIA

This is a very well-known superstition in Asia. The origin of this phobia toward the number four — this is what the term means — is in the fact that in Chinese, Japanese, Korean and Vietnamese, the word "death" is pronounced the same or similar to the number four.

Although its use is inevitable, people try to avoid using the number by taking the following measures:

- Number four is not mentioned in the presence of a sick person.
- In elevators, sometimes the number four is avoided (you go directly from floor three to five), especially in hospitals.
- People avoid having celebrations on the fourth day of each month.
- In China and Singapore, the number four is not used in serial numbers for airplanes, trains, ships and buses.

A study in the **British Medical Journal** that analyzed mortality statistics for Americans compared to Chinese and Japanese over a period of twenty-five years, concluded that Asians had a higher probability — up to thirty percent greater — of dying from a heart attack on the fourth day of each month compared to Americans (who are oblivious to tetraphobia)[1].

The results of the study were clear: the psychological stress caused by believing in the number four superstition may have fatal consequences. The psychosomatic mechanism by which stress is capable of increasing the chances of having a heart attack are still being studied.

Just as happens with other superstitions, it became a *self-fulfilling prophesy*. That is, **once a prediction has been made, it is in itself the cause of that event materializing**.

It is interesting to see the power that beliefs can have to influence the human psyche, both for good and for bad. If we are pessimistic, believing that **something bad** is going to happen to us will cause us stress and, as a consequence, the chances of something bad happening to us will be greater. If, on the other hand, we are optimistic and believe that **something good** is going to happen, that will free us from stress and fill us with hope.

---

1. Source, *British Medical Journal* study: https://pages.ucsd.edu/~dphillip/ baskerville.html

IF IT IS RED, IT BRINGS GOOD LUCK

Associated with good omens throughout the continent of Asia, **the color red is held in great esteem as one of the best kinds of good luck charm**. When the stock exchange is colored red in China, Japan or Korea, it doesn't mean shares are slumping — on the contrary, it means they are soaring.

Red is associated with abundance, money, power, love and even protection. You just need to take a look at the national flags of those three countries to realize that the color red is central to all of them. But where does this conviction that red brings good luck come from?

In China, the story goes that, hundreds of years ago, a mythical beast named Nian Shou was in the habit of spending the Chinese New Year devouring cattle and people. Luckily, someone discovered that Nian Shou was afraid of loud noises and the color red. From then on, it became a New Year tradition to light fireworks and to hang up red lanterns and auspicious messages on red paper in windows and doors. Nian Shou never came back, and to this day, red color rites still abound in China.

The traditional wedding dress for Chinese brides is not white but red. In addition, the Chinese New Year is celebrated by giving money in red envelopes.

The Japanese have a similar feeling toward the color red. It is the color of the *torii* — the entry gates to Shintoist shrines —since this hue is thought to be capable of **warding off evil spirits and affording protection, bringing peace, and conferring strength and power**. It is also considered the most cheerful color to wear, and **the combination of red and white is the most propitious** possible, as the choice of these colors for the country's flag shows.

Red also plays an important role in the predestination of the union between people, as described in **the legend of the red thread**. According to this Japanese myth, an old man who lives on the Moon comes out every night to look for kindred spirits so he may bring them together on Earth. When he finds people who have something to learn from one another, he ties them to a red thread so that their paths will cross. This is how our red threads come to end at another person, who will be a master to us. Acceptance of this can be a consolation since it implies we have never made bad decisions. Fate has brought us to exactly where we were supposed to be.

The most important red thread of all is the one that connects us to the person with whom we will experience the most important love story of our life. The thread starts at the pinkie, where the ulnar artery that comes directly from the heart leads, and ends at the other person's pinkie, from where it reaches their heart, thus binding together the two hearts forever.

The legend of the red thread is an invitation to understand our life as a predetermined storyline in which romances and other encounters we experience with others are not accidental. They are part of a scarlet plot whose threads were given to us at birth, but which we ourselves weave as we go along.

FUKUMIMI: LUCKY EARS

They say it is possible to predict how rich someone will be just by looking at their face — or, more exactly, their ears. It turns out there is a popular legend according to which there is a type that is especially fortunate.

Those ears are the ones with big fleshy lobes, known as *fukumimi* (福耳: lucky ears), which, moreover, are turned slightly upwards. Here in Japan, having *fukumimi* is a good omen, since it is deemed that you have been born with the potential to attract good fortune throughout your life.

The Seven Gods of Fortune have ears like that, with the ears of Daikokuten, the god of commerce and prosperity, being the most pronounced. Ebisu, the god of business, harvests and fishing, along with Hotei, the god of good fortune, also have this very noticeable characteristic. Popular culture has it that because the *fukumimi* earlobes are partially turned upwards, they form a kind of bowl that can hold a grain of rice, which means abundance is ever-present.

The *kanji* character of the words with favorable meanings like "sacred," "wise," or "wisdom" contains the root of the word "ear," reflecting the importance that is given to this characteristic in Japanese culture.

Buddha also has big-lobed ears, but in his case they point downwards and may be quite long. This kind of big but droopy earlobes is considered to be typical of a spiritual person, a saint or someone who simply has a good heart. We mustn't forget that Confucius also had this kind of ears.

Taking into account that *fukumimi* appear to be hereditary, we could come to the conclusion that the family into which we are born determines a large part of our destiny. Even so, no one ever said that not having this characteristic prevents you from becoming a prosperous person; **in the end, we weave our destiny day by day with good intentions and good actions**.

THE LUCKIEST OR UNLUCKIEST
TWO MEN IN THE WORLD

Among the league tables of people favored by chance, there are two names that always come to the fore, one Japanese and the other Croatian.

The first is Tsutomu Yamaguchi, the only person in history to have officially survived two nuclear bombs. Maybe it could be considered bad luck to have been in both places at the precise moment that each bomb fell, but it is miraculous is that he survived both events and lived to the age of ninety-three.

An engineer by profession, Yamaguchi went to Hiroshima for work on August 6th, 1945. The first nuclear bomb fell three kilometers from where he was, causing serious injuries to his entire body.

He took three days to recover slightly, after which he returned to his hometown — Nagasaki — where the second nuclear bomb fell on him; once again he was three kilometers away. Once again, he survived.

Yamaguchi devoted the rest of his life to giving talks, which he called "peace lessons," and to calling for nuclear disarmament. On his death, in 2010, the mayor of Nagasaki claimed that a great narrator of history had been lost.

Great as Yamaguchi's luck and destiny were, when people talk about "the luckiest man in the world," they tend to refer to Frane Selak, a Croat born in 1929, who would begin his idyll with fate in 1962.

That year he was traveling in a train when his coach derailed and fell into a river. Out of the eighteen passengers, seventeen drowned. Frane alone escaped, merely suffering a fractured arm.

The following year, in his first — and last — airplane trip, an onboard explosion blew the door off the plane, and Frane was ejected into the air. Miraculously, he escaped death once more by falling onto the hay loft of a farm, while the rest of the airplane passengers died.

In 1966, he would survive a bus accident, when a bus also fell into a river and four passengers died.

In 1970, his automobile caught fire while he was driving, but he managed to get out seconds before the fuel tank exploded.

Three years later, his hair caught fire due to another fire in his car, but he didn't suffer any serious injuries.

His next stroke of luck came along in 1995, when he was run over by a bus in Zagreb, but got away with only minor injuries.

A year later, a multiple collision caused by a United Nations truck on a bend of a mountain road forced him to leap out of his vehicle, which he was able to do thanks to the fact he wasn't wearing his seatbelt. His automobile fell ninety meters into a ravine, but he escaped the fall by hanging onto a tree.

Seeing all of these terrible encounters with death, we might consider Selak the unluckiest man in the world, but the fact he escaped death seven times s evidence of the contrary.

Topping it all off, in 2003, two days after celebrating his seventy-fourth birthday, he won 800,000 euros in the lottery. After buying two houses and a rowboat, he donated the rest of the money to his family and friends and lived a simple life until the day he died — of natural causes — at the age of eighty-six.

Legend has it that Bodhidharma meditated for nine years without moving.

DARUMA

*"Believe in others,
but believe in yourself a hundred times more."*
—JAPANESE PROVERB

Daruma dolls look like misshapen eggs and are most commonly painted red with a white face portraying Bodhidharma.

The story of the historic character is a mixture of fantasy, legend and mythology.

Bodhidharma is thought to be the first monk to have conveyed the Buddhist tradition to China. From the Indian subcontinent, he traveled to China, where he trained in a Shaolin monastery. Later, he carried on traveling until he entered a cave and set to meditating while looking at a wall for nine years.

The legend goes that he closed his eyes just once and became so angry with himself, because of his lack of discipline, that he cut off his eyelids. When his eyelids fell to the ground, green tea plants sprouted forth. This myth is one of the reasons why people in Japan drink green tea to stay awake.

According to myth, after so many years spent meditating without moving, the monk lost his arms and legs. This is the reason why Daruma dolls have no limbs.

These figures are used as good luck talismans, but also symbolize other values associated with the legend:

- **Perseverance and patience:** if you feel disheartened and have lost your drive and motivation, remember that Bodhidharma spent nine years without moving. That will help you to put your situation into perspective.
- **Resilience:** a well-designed *daruma* doll rebounds and returns to its original position when you tilt it. If you don't succeed at first, keep trying.
- **Discipline:** if you are sufficiently disciplined to get what you wish for, perhaps you will have to sacrifice certain things, but that will make you feel free. Decide carefully what you are willing to make sacrifices for and be disciplined about it.
- **Happiness with nothing:** if you feel frustrated because you didn't get something material, remember that Bodhidharma was content with nothing. He only possessed a red habit.

The important thing if we mean to get what we desire is not simply to leave things to chance. In order for fate to be under our control, we must apply patience, discipline and perseverance. This message is the essence of the Japanese proverb *nanakorobiyaoki* 七転び八起き: "*If you fall seven times, get up eight*," which is often written in traditional Japanese calligraphy beside daruma dolls.

HOW TO USE A *DARUMA DOLL*

1) When you buy a *daruma*, you will notice its eyes are not painted.

2) You have to paint one of its eyes and at the same time set yourself a new life goal.

3) Put the doll in a place where you will be able to see it every day. It will serve as a reminder to you that you haven't achieved your goal yet and have to keep working at it.

4) Although you may take some time to achieve it, the *daruma* will help you to not get disheartened. Remember that the *daruma* only helps those who are steadfast and make sacrifices for what they most want.

5) Once you have achieved your goal, you may paint the second eye. With that, you are giving thanks to Bodhidharma for having helped you with what you had set your mind to.

6) If you bought the *daruma* at a temple, you have to return it there, where it will be burned following a traditional ritual.

Daruma *dolls on sale (Still without the eyes painted) at the entrance to a temple.*
© Hector Garcia

THE OLD MAN AND HIS WANDERING HORSE

*"For there is nothing either good or bad,
but thinking makes it so"*

—HAMLET, WILLIAM SHAKESPEARE[1]

This is a very popular Taoist tale throughout Asia. In Japan, we have a popular proverb that refers directly to the story:

"Everything in life is like the old man's horse at the border."
人間万事塞翁が馬

And here is the tale:

Good and bad luck change from one into the other and
it is hard to tell when this is going to happen.
A man lived next to the border.
His horse escaped and reached barbarian territory.
Everyone felt sorry for him.
His father said to him: "Who knows if this will bring
you good luck?"

---

1. https://books.google.co.jp/books?id=Rps0AAAAMAAJ&pg=PA35&redir_esc=y#v=onepage&q&f=false

Months later, the horse came back along with a group
of several of the barbarians' horses.

Everyone congratulated him.

His father said to him: "Who knows if this will bring
you bad luck?"

The son mounted one of the new horses eagerly.

But he fell off and broke a leg.

Everyone felt sorry for him.

His father said to him: "Who knows if this will bring
you good luck?"

A year later, the barbarians crossed the border and
invaded.

The healthy adult men fought and nine out of ten of
them died.

Since the son had a broken leg, he couldn't fight. That
saved him.

Both father and son *survived*.

Bad luck brings good luck,

and good luck brings bad luck again.

This always happens, unendingly,

and no one can predict changes.

The purpose of this parable is to make us reflect on how
we should react to and interpret what at first we consider good
or bad luck. **We should not rush to interpret either the good
or bad things that happen to us. It is important to keep an
even-minded attitude.**

Each time something good or bad happens to the protag-
onist, his father makes him reflect with a question. This question helps him to maintain a neutral outlook, come what may.

Sometimes, the best things in life come after a setback. And when everything is going well, maybe the next thing will be bad news. The key is to accept this good-bad sequence as something that has always been common in human experience.

True happiness comes from accepting life just as it is.

SHINTOIST RITUALS FOR A GOOD LIFE

Shintoism is a millenary life philosophy that currently coexists with Buddhism in Japan. Along with other animist religions, **Shintoism bases its beliefs on the existence of spirits in everything that surrounds us**.

According to this tradition, human beings come into this world pure, in what is known as a *kami* state, and our mission in life is to stay as close as possible to this state.

The experiences we have over our lifetime through our six "organs" —nose, eyes, ears, mouth, body, mind —, lead to us accumulating *kegare*, or impurities, which we must become conscious of in order to cleanse them and transcend.

With this aim in mind, there are some Shintoist rituals we can carry out at home. Practicing them will help us to transform *kegare* and bring us closer to the desired state of *kami*, full of purity:

1. **The salt ritual.** The power of salt to act as a deterrent to bad energy is known to the cultures throughout the world. Shintoism is no exception, and has a couple of different salt rituals depending on what we are going to purify.
    a. To promote clean energy at home or in business premises, it is traditional to put salt in two bowls by the front door.

    b. Sumo is very popular in Japan. Prior to becoming a sport, it was a Shintoist tradition. Before each combat begins, the wrestlers throw salt on the ground to scare away evil spirits. At the same time, they also throw salt at their feet because it is useful as a disinfectant if they get scratched.

2. **The nature ritual.** In nature, there live many benign spirits since it is their favorite habitat. The well-known Japanese forest bathing — *shinrin yoku* — which has been a part of Japan's national health plan since 1982, is one of Shintoists' favorite rituals for discarding heavy daily burdens and for coming ever closer to the pure state in which we came into this world. Contact with nature eliminates impurities and recharges our life force.

2. **The appreciation ritual.** Being grateful brings us closer to *kami*. In Japanese, the expression ***itadakimasu*** is used before meals as a sign of gratitude for the food, and also when receiving something, like a gift. This expression is a sign of respect and gratitude to all those who have contributed to the food reaching your plate, from the farmer to the cook, and encompasses the favorable meteorological conditions that helped make it possible for you to enjoy it. This practice of the recognition of other people's efforts places us a little closer to the divine plane, in so far as it makes us like a child who accepts things with open arms and a smile on their face.

There are other Shintoist rituals that can only be carried out in shrines, which is why, if you visit Japan, you must take advantage of the opportunity these rituals afford you to attract good fortune.

One of the most popular rites consists of writing a wish on a wooden *ema* plaque, as we saw in the chapter dedicated to them. Although it is common to do this at New Year, it may be carried out any time. These plaques are everywhere, and any shrine will give you the chance to get your hands on one that you can hang up with your wish. It is said the wish will come true before the following New Year.

Another tradition you can follow when visiting temples or shrines on your trip around Japan is to buy *omikuji*. The *omikuji* is a kind of personal fortune written on a piece of paper. Although most *omikuji* are in Japanese, it is also possible to find them in English in the temples that are big tourist attractions.

If you have bad luck when you buy omikuji, custom dictates that you must fold it and tie it to a string at the same temple where you bought it. © Hector Garcia

Zeniarai Benten: the money-multiplying temple

A Spanish friend of mine called Javier came to visit me and to travel around Japan in 2009. He spent a day getting to know Kamakura, where he visited the Zenarai Bentenshrine. "Zenarai" literally means "to wash coins" and Benten is the name of a Buddhist goddess.

According to belief, if you wash money in the shrine fountain, your wealth will multiply in the future. People visit the shrine and wash all kinds of things connected to money, from coins and bills to stock exchange contracts in order to attract good financial fortune.

My friend Javier is not at all superstitious, and I would say he's very skeptical, but even he washed a thousand yen bill during his visit. Years later, he and his partner Emilio sold their startup for several million euros.

CATS AND LUCK

For Spanish people, it is bad luck to cross paths with a black cat. However, in other cultures, cats, including black ones, are seen as creatures that offer protection against bad luck.

It is well known that in Ancient Egypt cats were regarded as sacred animals and were treated almost like gods. The ancient Egyptian goddess Bastet, Ra's daughter, had a cat's face and was the goddess of love, joy, protection, dance and — obviously — cats. The Egyptians believed that cats' eyes reflected the sun's rays, thus protecting the people in the villages where they lived from darkness and misfortune.

In India and China there were feline goddesses of fertility: Sastht and Li Chou, respectively.

Celtic folklore includes a great black cat — *the king of the cats* — called Irusan, capable of blessing those who treated him with respect. And the Vikings adored their cat goddess of love and beauty, Freya.

In Ancient Japan, cats were revered and kept in pagodas, where they guarded priceless manuscripts. In fact, they were considered so valuable in the tenth century that only members of the nobility were allowed to own them.

Buddhist culture believes cats are sacred creatures, since they regard them as one of the most aware animals. Buddhist monks say cats act as hosts for certain sacred human souls after death. These souls of people who have attained the highest level of enlightenment supposedly return to the Earth for the last time as a cat, with the soul being released in order to reach nirvana at the end of the cat's life.

Even today, in the county of Yorkshire, England, it is good luck to have black cats as pets as they are considered to be particularly auspicious for ensuring sailors return home safe and sound. Not very far from there, in Scotland, coming across a black street cat under your house porch indicates that good fortune will soon arrive.

There is also a commonly held belief, not only among the Japanese, but among anyone who has a hint of the sixth sense, that having cats at home removes bad energy since cats absorb and transform it. It is not uncommon to see a cat settle onto its owner's lap when they have had a bad day, with the intention of freeing them of their malaise, which the cat transmutes by its mere presence.

In any case, the cat is probably the most feared and at the same time the most revered animal for a variety of superstitions. Perhaps, quite simply, everything depends on how you decide to see it. **What you believe, you create**.

HOW MANY LIVES DOES A CAT HAVE?

"Cats have seven lives in Arab countries and in Turkey; seven in Latin America and Portugal; nine where the language of Shakespeare is spoken. Why does a cat need so many lives?

An old English proverb explains it like this:

In the first three it plays.
In the next three it roams around the streets.
And in the last three it stays at home."

From the novel *Neko Cafe'* by Anna Sólyom

THE MANEKI NEKO'S SEVEN LAWS

I shall finish this journey with a brief summary of some concepts — laws if you like — that we have discussed in this book. However, before that, I want to share this table, which is for choosing the polarity you want to live by.

+ To attract luck	– To remain bogged down in a boring life without luck
You learn and study new things every day.	You stop learning.
Curiosity	Passivity, apathy and indifference
You interact with people who have varied interests.	You only speak to people who think the same as you.
Optimism	Pessimism
Faced with a stroke of bad luck you recover right away and try again.	You lose heart at the first setback on your path.
You present your creations to the world and help others.	You keep everything to yourself and only look after number one.

+ To attract luck	– To remain bogged down in a boring life without luck
You are eager to learn new things.	You feel apathy toward any novelty that may appear in your life that doesn't form part of your routine.
You know how to detect good opportunities.	Opportunities pass right by you without you noticing them.

In the light of this, let's look at **the Maneki Neko's seven laws** for preparing the ground for good fortune:

1
Study the laws of luck
Not everything is random — you must take control of what depends upon you.

2
Apply ganbatte
Knowledge is infertile if it is not accompanied by effort and constant action.

3
Believe it to create it
Confidence is a fundamental ingredient in making it possible for good fortune to materialize.

4
Take a chance on optimism
A positive expectation about your chances
increases the probability of success.

5
Practice resilience
Fortune favors those people
who do not tire of hard work.

6
Surround yourself with people who empower you
A nourishing environment will help you to achieve
any plan you have set you mind to.

7
Follow your curiosity
With an explorer's spirit,
you will discover the best opportunities.

All the best,
happy life adventures
and good luck with your good luck,

NOBUO SUZUKI

BIBLIOGRAPHY

Austin, James H., *Chase, Chance, and Creativity: The Lucky Art of Novelty*, MIT Press

Benito, Cristina, *Money Mindfulness*, Grijalbo

Byrne, Rondha, *The Secret*, Urano

DiCicco, Sue and Masahiro Sasaki, *The Complete Story of Sadako Sasaki*, Tuttle Publishing

Christakis, Nicholas A. & James H. Fowler, *Connected: The Surprising Power of Our Social Networks and How They Shape Our Lives*, Taurus

Emoto, Masaru, *The Hidden Messages in Water*, Fontanar

Kiyosaki, Robert, *Rich Dad Poor Dad*, DeBolsillo

Rovira, Álex & Fernando Trías de Bes, *La Buena Suerte*, Zenith

Sólyom, Anna, *Neko Café*, Universo

Takayuki, Ishii, *One Thousand Paper Cranes: The Story of Sadako and the Children's Peace Statue*, Nube de Tinta

Taleb, Nassim Nicolas, *Fooled by Randomness: The Hidden Role of Chance in Life and in the Markets*, Booket

Trismegisto, Hermes, *The Kybalion*, Sirio

Tsunemoto, Yamamoto, *Hagakure: the Secret Wisdom of the Samurai*, translated by Alex Bennett, Tuttle Publishing

Vives, Xenia, *Tener Suerte en la Vida Depende de TMasahiroi*, Aguilar

"Books to Span the East and West"

Tuttle Publishing was founded in 1832 in the small New England town of Rutland, Vermont [USA]. Our core values remain as strong today as they were then—to publish best-in-class books which bring people together one page at a time. In 1948, we established a publishing outpost in Japan—and Tuttle is now a leader in publishing English-language books about the arts, languages and cultures of Asia. The world has become a much smaller place today and Asia's economic and cultural influence has grown. Yet the need for meaningful dialogue and information about this diverse region has never been greater. Over the past seven decades, Tuttle has published thousands of books on subjects ranging from martial arts and paper crafts to language learning and literature—and our talented authors, illustrators, designers and photographers have won many prestigious awards. We welcome you to explore the wealth of information available on Asia at **www.tuttlepublishing.com**.

Published by Tuttle Publishing, an imprint of Periplus Editions (HK) Ltd.

www.tuttlepublishing.com

Published in Spain as *Maneki Neko: il Libro Japonés de la Buena Fortuna* by Ediciones Obelisco © 2023 by Nobuo Suzuki
Translation © 2023 by Periplus Editions, (HK) Ltd.
Translated from Spanish by Russell Andrew Calvert
Translation rights arranged by Sandra Bruna Agencia Literaria, SL.

Library of Congress publication data is in progress.

ISBN: 978-4-8053-1737-2

26 25 24 23   10 9 8 7 6 5 4 3 2 1
Printed in Malaysia   2304VP

Distributed by
North America, Latin America & Europe
Tuttle Publishing
364 Innovation Drive
North Clarendon
VT 05759-9436 U.S.A.
Tel: (802) 773-8930; Fax: (802) 773-6993
info@tuttlepublishing.com
www.tuttlepublishing.com

Japan
Tuttle Publishing
Yaekari Building 3rd Floor
5-4-12 Osaki Shinagawa-ku
Tokyo 141 0032
Tel: (81) 3 5437-0171; Fax: (81) 3 5437-0755
sales@tuttle.co.jp
www.tuttle.co.jp

Asia Pacific
Berkeley Books Pte. Ltd.
3 Kallang Sector #04-01
Singapore 349278
Tel: (65) 6741-2178; Fax: (65) 6741-2179
inquiries@periplus.com.sg
www.tuttlepublishing.com

TUTTLE PUBLISHING® is a registered trademark of Tuttle Publishing, a division of Periplus Editions (HK) Ltd.